ASTERIA

POETRY COLLECTION

GW00384566

EMMA DOE

ASTERIA
POETRY COLLECTION

To my grandparents, *Joseph Richard Gascoyne,* and *Kathleen Mary Gascoyne* – thank you for believing in my dreams. Thank you for loving and supporting my poetry throughout the previous years.

Grandad – I hope that you read this first published collection of my poetry and still have that same twinkle in your eyes as you wear that proud smile. You inspire me every day.

Nanna – I hope that my words find their way to you beyond the moon and past the stars. I know that you would have loved this book, you always loved my poetry. I think of you every day.

I love you both. You were the first readers of my poetry and I dedicate Asteria to both of you.

To you – the reader. Thank you for believing in an unknown author. My hope is, on rainy days or during sleepless nights, that you find my first published collection of poetry to be as alluring as Greek mythology and as beguiling as the goddesses themselves. All nine goddesses starring in this collection have a story to tell. Thank you for listening to them.

And final thanks to – caffeine and Taylor Swift vinyl records, for keeping me soaring amongst the stars..........
no matter the late-night hour.

☾

"I've dreamt in my life dreams that have stayed with me ever after, and changed my ideas; they've gone through and through me, like wine through water, and altered the colour of my mind."

- Emily Brontë, Wuthering Heights

"According to Greek Mythology, humans were originally created with four arms, four legs and a head with two faces. Fearing their power, Zeus split them into two separate beings, condemning them to spend their lives in search of their other halves."

- Plato, The Symposium

CONTENTS

FOREWORD

Ancient Greek goddesses are both powerful and resonant, even today, in the twenty first century. Every goddess is cloaked with mythological stories of lust, love, heartbreak, hurting, healing, fate, destiny, life, death and so much more. The fascinating stories of these ancient Greek goddesses are embedded within the pages of so many books, books just like Asteria, that are yearning to be read.

My aim with *Asteria* was to bring these goddesses to life once again through 180 rhymed poems. Each of the nine chapters relate to one particular goddess, with the poems from her chapter unravelling her own mythology whilst also unveiling her own unique story. Asteria reveals her primary association with a single human emotion, feeling and experience that is still relatable even today, almost 3,000 years later. Every rhymed poem has been delicately interwoven with the mythology of the following nine ancient Greek goddesses, some you may already be aware of, others may be new to you, but they all have a story to tell, if you have the time to hear them.

As the goddess of lust, *Siren* relates to themes of lust, seduction, compulsion, deceit, and betrayal. As the goddess of woe, *Oizys* relates to themes of woe, heartbreak, grief, misery, and sadness. As the goddess of love, *Aphrodite* relates to themes of love, beauty, jealousy, envy, and passion. As the goddess of life and death, *Persephone* relates to themes of life, death, sacrifice, and obsession. As the goddesses of fate, *The Fates* relates to themes of fate, destiny, mortality, and soul mates. As the goddess of the fallen star, *Asteria* relates to themes of the stars and their connection to the soul. As the goddess of the moon, *Selene* relates to themes of the moon, darkness, and dreams. As the goddess of night, *Nyx* relates to themes of solitude, darkness, evil, and the unseen. As the goddess of magic, *Circe* relates to themes of magic, unrequited love, bitterness, temptation and the unknown. Welcome to Asteria.

SIREN

THE STORY OF SIREN

Meet Peisinoe, Agalope, and Thelxiepeia,
The siren sisters three,
Half birds, half beautiful maidens,
Who dwell on rocks amidst the sea.

These mythological creatures,
Were the daughters of a muse.
The embodiment of desire and lust,
They lure any man they choose.

The trio sang a woeful song,
That enchant the wind and sea,
And any man who heard their voice,
Fell prey to melody.

The embodiment of lust and sex,
Men sought for their caress,
For they sang hauntingly beautiful,
With a voice that could possess.

The sirens draw them in by voice,
And lead them to their fate,
Compelling them to steer their ships,
To the rocks where they await.

The shipwrecked boats lay dormant,
As no man survives their call,
Once you hear the song of sirens,
You shall crash, and drown, then fall.

ODYSSEUS

Odysseus had left the arms of Circe,
Despite her plea,
But she warned him of the dangers,
That await him on the sea.

'You will soon encounter Sirens,
And their potent song allures,
You must close your ears my darling,
Or your death these creatures cause'.

Despite his lovers warning,
Odysseus prepared to sail,
How he longed to hear the Sirens song,
But live to tell the tale.

His crew were given beeswax,
That would block the ears of all,
But he had them bind him to the mast,
With his ears free for their call.

Once he heard the Sirens voices,
He begged hard to be untied,
But the beeswax blocked their hearing,
And they sailed on and survived.

Now legend spoke of Sirens,
How their deaths would come to be,
Should anyone survive their song,
They shall hurl themselves to sea.

SIREN SONG

The trio sing a melancholic,
Tune that trance the sea.
A pensive song of lustfulness,
With words of potency.

The men who heard their chorus,
Were compelled without a choice,
To steer towards the ones they hear,
Impelled by Sirens voice.

The song spoke of the heartache,
For the lovers been betrayed,
By the lustful sailors drawn to them,
Each time they would serenade.

The words concealed the loneliness,
Each one conveyed the woe,
That the trio felt upon the rocks,
Each time the men would show.

The song would lure the passing ships,
Towards the Sirens three,
So close but yet so far away,
They would lose them to the sea.

The sirens curse, of loneliness,
Etched by the Fates decree.

SAILOR

There is an island in the sea,
There, live the siren sisters, three.
One strums a golden harp, the lyre,
One sings a song of pure desire,
The third, she plays a silver flute,
The ones who hear the three, re-route,
Towards the source, the sailors go,
Towards their deaths, how could they know?
So bewitched and so entranced,
So enraptured they advanced.
Before the lustful held their gaze,
Before they drowned in crashing waves,
The last thing that the sailors saw,
The Sirens, creatures of the lore,
They sat and watched the sailors yield,
They paused a while, and smiles revealed,
That every man had drowned at sea,
That death elate the Sirens, three.

ZEPHYR

The sea is calm, serene, and clear,
As she sings to zephyr sky,
She charms the wind and water,
With her woeful lullaby.

The sun burns brightly overhead,
As the breeze kisses her skin.
Her hair cascades behind her,
As her song draws sailors in.

The ship drifts effervescently,
To the rock she occupies,
As the men aboard the vessel,
Are fixated by her cries.

The men are ever closer,
But little did they know,
It was not a song of beauty,
But a fatal tale of woe.

The zephyr sky then dissipates,
For storm clouds overhead,
As she smiles with every crashing ship,
And she welcomes in the dead.

LYRE LIAR

She plays her lyre,
A golden harp,
And as her fingers strum,
Her melody is cast to sea,
Ensuring ships succumb.
Her lyre lies,
To bring demise,
To its tune,
All men shall come.

No ship, nor man, evades them,
When she plays the lyres hum.

She enchants the wind,
Controls the sea,
And floods the ears of all,
Who hear the song, the Siren sings,
To draw them to her call.
She lures them in,
And once within,
Her grasp,
Each man shall fall.

No ship, nor man, survives the wreck,
To the lyre they are in thrall.

DRAWN TO HER CALL

The midnight sky is velvet black,
Pressed with abundant stars,
And on a rock in Anthemusa,
She sings her song of scars.

She tells a tale of tragedy,
Of pain and disbelief,
Of loneliness and broken hearts,
But beyond all this, of grief.

Her grief comes from the heartache,
Of lovers been betrayed,
By her song and its enchantment,
Over lustful men who strayed.

Men who failed to close their ears,
Were drawn to Siren's call,
Her words held potent warnings,
That they failed to hear at all.

She cast her voice to sea and sky,
To lure all wicked men,
And all those drawn to Siren's call,
Were never seen again.

THE ROSE

You plant a rose within my heart,
With a scent of sweet perfume,
Epitomizing love, and trust,
Ensuring both would bloom.

The rose that you instilled in me,
Unfurled its crimson hue,
Every root embedded fervently,
Till my heart beat just for you.

The rose bloomed more seductively,
Each time my heart would beat,
But beneath its aesthetic,
Lay the truth of our deceit.

The rose concealed a secret,
Only you and I had known,
That it represented secret love,
From a seed we both had sown.

You plant a rose within my heart,
Each thorn pierced me with guilt,
Alike the rose that blooms and grows,
Our love was doomed to wilt.

ANCHOR

'Lay down your anchor darling,
For I shall be your home,
No longer lost amidst the sea,
You shall not be alone,
I promise I shall love you,
For now, and evermore,
Lay down your anchor darling,
And join me on the shore.'

'I lay down my anchor darling,
So enamored by your gaze,
The ardent fire within your eyes,
Entrance me as it blaze,
You promised you would love me,
As our flames of ardor flash,
I lay down my anchor darling,
Then watched the embers turn to ash.'

HALF-PARTED LIPS

How beautiful, the siren,
With her hair in tousled waves,
Who sings her captivating song,
To lure sailors to their graves.

Her voice is so beguiling,
One to make them change their course,
As their minds are overpowered,
By desire to find the source.

Her song spills from half-parted lips,
The story of her woe,
A tragic tale of loneliness,
That the sailors wish to know.

Her eyes are filled with half tears,
As her song enchants the sea,
And the ships of men entranced by her,
Hit the rocks on which she be.

Her words brought on the death of those,
Who fell for her allure,
As she sits, surrounded by decay,
Where she sings her song, once more.

ABANDON SHIP

I wait for you, my sailor,
Believing you shall come,
Illicitly, complicity,
You always were the one.

I yearn for you, my sailor,
And your promise to propose,
Infallibly, unfailingly,
I dream of you when in repose.

I long for you, my sailor,
So, I promise I shall wait,
Devotedly, decidedly,
Our threads are bound by fate.

I ache for you, my sailor,
For without you I despair,
Abandon ship, my sailor,
When you do, I shall be there.

ENCHANTED

A satin gown clung to her skin,
And draped across her hips,
It was siren red and lustrous,
And its hue paired with her lips.

She would tempt them with her body,
As their needs she could fulfil,
She would tease them and appease them,
Till each man bent to her will.

Her lips were plump and sensual,
She was the embodiment of lust,
Every man that she enchanted,
Each betray their pledge of trust.

Each man that touched her body,
Elicit flames of pure desire,
But the ones who fell for her allure,
Strayed too close to the fire.

Seldom, did a man evade her gaze,
And both their eyes would clash,
Yet short lived was their adultery,
As the flames soon turned to ash.

SEDUCTION

She beckons him towards her,
Intent to bend his will,
So wild, the fire that burns for him,
That her mind would not be still.

She spoke of lustful reverie,
Intent she would appease,
So warm the fire that he inspired,
He brought her to her knees.

She kissed him with such passion,
Intent on their embrace.
So strong the fire from her desire,
That her tongue craved for his taste.

She bedded him with ardor,
Intent their flame would last,
So fueled the fire that she admire,
That burned and crackled vast.

She held him close with longing,
Intent he would not stray,
So stoked the fire that he inspire,
That would make him want to stay.

SIRENS KISS

The Sirens kiss is potent,
One that no man can resist,
Consumed by lustful thoughts of her,
From the moment that they kissed.

Her lips have such intensity,
With the power to appease,
Alluring and ensuring,
That all men fall to their knees.

She wore a crimson lipstick,
To entice through its allure,
Appealing and intriguing,
To each man that she would lure.

Her kiss was not insatiable,
To those who felt the taste,
She beguiled men, as she smiled,
When both their lips, at last, embrace.

A warning comes with Siren's kiss:
But for her, all shall efface.

MEADOW OF FLOWERS

On the island of Anthemusa,
Lived the Sirens,
Legend told,
That the banks were starred with flowers,
Unfurling fragrance as they strolled.

The sun burned bright in Anthemusa,
Over flowers,
Bright and bold,
Adding beauty to the landscape,
With each petal that unfold.

But there are secrets in Anthemusa,
Lying dormant,
Tales untold,
Beneath the banks of fragrant flowers,
Lay bones and corpses, cold.

The three sirens of Anthemusa,
Lure the sailors,
To their hold,
Under their spell, each sailor dies,
But efflorescence obscures the mould.

WRECKAGE

She sits alone,
Surrounded,
By the wreckage of your lust,
You broke her heart,
It shattered,
And the debris turned to rust.

She sheds her tears,
They overspill,
By the shipwreck of your lies,
You broke her trust,
Deceived her,
And the pain spills from her eyes.

She drowns in tears,
Of silence,
By the ruin you had brought.
Smooth sailing turned,
To chaos,
And the wreckage leaves her fraught.

DROWNING

He is drowning,
Falling, falling,
Deeper, deeper,
Down he goes.
He had heard you,
Heard you calling,
Lustful words,
To songs he knows.

He is drowning,
Falling, falling,
Deeper, deeper,
In the blue.
He is bidding,
Bidding farewell,
To the life,
That he once knew.

He is drowning,
Falling, falling,
Deeper, deeper,
Over you,
As his sight dims,
Dims to darkness,
Dousing flames,
His eyes once knew.

EPHEMERAL

She longs for him to hear her song,
That is carried on the breeze,
The song of immorality,
That will bring him to his knees.

She aches to sing the words to him,
Of a song to make him stray,
The one that overpowers the guilt,
For the one he will betray.

She desires for him to hold her,
To place his hands upon her hips,
To fuel the fire of pure desire,
Then kiss her eager lips.

She yearns for him to want her.
Lustful thoughts she has in mind,
She envisions him inside her,
Both their bodies intertwined.

She wishes to seduce him,
To entrance him with her eyes,
But she knows this is ephemeral,
Nothing lasts when built on lies.

WHISKEY WORDS

Whiskey words – unfiltered –
Form intoxicated scripts,
Lustful, spoken thoughts, that spill,
Through Bourbon coated lips.

Whiskey words – enveloping –
Form unintended lies,
Seductive, longing looks, observed,
Through liquor veiled eyes.

Whiskey words – disclosing –
Form bodies, intertwined,
Impassioned, longed for touch, desired,
Through drunk and hazy mind.

Whiskey words – unbounded –
Form undisclosed deceit,
Temporal passion, attained, enthralled,
Through inebriated heat.

Whiskey words – impermanent –
Form convoluted rue,
The moon descends, the mind amends,
Through sobered point of view.

EPIPHANY

Every word you said to me,

Promise that you made,

Ignite a fire within my heart,

Preserved, it should not fade.

Hopeful, that our love would last,

As both our hearts entwine,

Now I see the epiphany,

You were never truly mine.

'Do you hear the Siren song?
Beware her fatal call,
For the lustful and the wicked,
Are innately cursed to fall.'

OIZYS

THE STORY OF OIZYS

Meet Oizys, but with a caution,
Before all meet her, you should know,
She is the goddess of pure misery,
And her tale comes cloaked in woe.

Her father was Erebus,
And her mother's name was Nyx,
Erebus was the God of dark,
And Nyx, the goddess of eclipse.

She had a brother, Momus,
Her twin was evil too,
Whilst she was goddess of misery,
He was the God of blame and rue.

There are barely any stories,
Told about Oizys,
For those who speak her name aloud,
Are scared, and feared, and quiesce.

Oizys is the embodiment,
Of misery and pain,
Of heartbreak, grief, and sadness,
And her reign shall never wane.

She was born with evil intentions,
Towards humanity,
Tread carefully around Oizys,
A goddess without mythology.

KINTSUGI

You are beautiful, but broken,
Your pain echoes through each tear,
I can feel the words unspoken,
But I promise you, I am here.

There is an art-form called Kintsugi,
It is something rare and true,
Where they piece back something broken,
Using gold, each piece they glue.

Take comfort from this metaphor,
For once you are restored,
You shall embrace your beauty,
And accept we all are flawed.

You will be stronger than you have ever known,
And this shall never fade,
You shall be unique and beautiful,
Something gold and fragments made.

So wipe your tears, my darling,
For the words I say are true,
There is no other on this earth,
Who is as strong,

As you.

LIGHTHOUSE

I'm in the darkness,
In the shadows,
Sometimes lost, sometimes alone,
And I cry into my pillow,
Often times when on my own.

But I am like a lighthouse,
As I stand amidst the dark,
And I guide the way of others,
With a light formed from a spark.

This light derives from courage,
And it is bright enough to guide,
As I ease the pain of others,
And I cast my own aside.

It is strength that keeps me glowing,
And compassion sees me through,
For I know the pain of shadows,
As I'm lost within them too.

So, although I stand in darkness,
I shall shine beyond my fear,
And just alike the lighthouse,
I will be strong,

And always here.

TELL HER

Tell her how you hold me,
How you long for time to pause,
That when I'm wrapped within your arms,
You pretend that I am yours.

Tell her how you kiss me,
How your tongue caresses mine,
That when I'm stood beside you,
You know our hearts align.

Tell her how you touch me,
How you are lost within my gaze,
That when I'm laid beside you,
You can feel the heat we blaze.

Tell her how you want me,
How you ache for me each night,
That when I'm holding onto you,
You hold me back so tight.

And tell her how you miss me,
How you wish time could rewind,
For when I'm not there with you,
You have only me in mind,

For we both are tangled in a web of lies,

We each,

Designed.

DEAR YOU

This letter holds the hardest words,
I've ever had to write,
To you, the one I loved, so true,
You, who set my heart alight.

My tears spill on the paper,
As I pen the words goodbye,
And though I long to tear it up,
I know I need to try.

I need to say these words to you,
For beyond the way I feel,
You offered love, then broke my heart,
Now it needs the time to heal.

I love you, and the hardest,
Words to say, shall be goodbye,
And the ink spills from the tears I shed,
As I sit, and write, and cry.

My heart aches with every syllable,
The pen trembles in my hand,
I do not want to say goodbye,

I don't,

But I hope you understand.

CORDOLIUM

Cordolium, is heartfelt grief,
Or sorrow of the heart,
It comes almost intuitively,
At the moment lovers part.

It is inevitable, for many,
Unavoidable, for some,
It cannot be evaded,
From this pain you cannot run.

It quells you into silence,
Into crying tears at night,
And it makes you feel so powerless,
Too strong for you to fight.

It has no sound, *Cordolium,*
When your heart breaks, no one hears,
So you relieve this painful feeling,
The only way you can, through tears.

But there is a light, so blinding,
And in time, your pain shall flee,
We each have to go through heartbreak,
To see what love can be.

LOSING YOU

The sky lost all its stars at once,
That night you said goodbye,
I watched as each one faded,
I was heartbroken, and jaded,
Gazing at an empty sky.

The moon seemed sympathetic,
As she dimmed her lunar glow,
I watched as she illuminate,
I lost all faith I had in fate,
And my tears overflow.

The air turned cold and bitter,
And it froze my heart to ice,
The chill was almost numbing,
For the pain of our shortcoming,
Meant our love was not suffice.

The world all slept in silence,
But my thoughts would not be quelled,
They were racing, interlacing,
Replacing, then misplacing,
Not one memory was withheld.

I lost half of my heart that night,
When I let you walk away,
I watched your silhouette in view,
Until there was no trace of you,
I just could not make you stay

SHINY BROKEN PIECES

She was shiny broken pieces,

Her mosaic of her past,

Interwoven memories, from love,

Not meant to last.

You can see them pieced together,

Broken pieces now restored,

Rearranged, and each one changed,

One heart, beautiful, but flawed.

Kindness seemed to be her downfall,

Each man would come and then depart,

Never knowing that their cruelty, would,

Perforate her heart.

Inner thoughts would then invade her,

Every night she lay to sleep,

Consumed her mind, till she resigned,

Each man would soon leave her behind,

She would overthink and weep.

BOKETTO

She was Boketto,
-Looking forwards-
As she gaze without a thought,
Tears were forming,
And were falling,
The only sign,
That she was fraught.

She was gazing with such heavy eyes,
-That blurred-
The view ahead,
And she was lost,
Within the silence,
Not one thought,
Ran through her head.

She was frozen in a memory,
-And lost-
No longer could she see,
As she gaze,
Out in the distance,
With her mind,
Hollow, empty.

She was Boketto,
-Looking forwards-
But not gazing at the view,
She was broken,
Her mind empty,
Till every trace,
Had gone, of you.

TORN

I am torn, my heart is broken,
I know that what we have is true,
I feel it, every time we speak,
And I know that you do too.

But you listen to their voices,
And believe the words they say,
Even though you know you love me,
You pull yourself away.

It hurts me, and it breaks my heart,
I wish that you were here,
And I'm so confused, do you choose,
Avoidance just from fear?

There was an age – old fable,
Penned by someone great,
And he wrote of Romeo and Juliet,
Two lovers bound by fate.

But they, like us, were parted,
As each were pulled away,
And I wish and hope with longing heart,
You and I can find a way.

UNREQUITED

He does not see me,
Though I see him,
I am invisible, you see,
For when I gaze into his eyes,
His own see straight through me.

He does not need me,
Though I need him,
Unrequited, you could say,
For when I reach out for his hand,
He pulls his own away.

He does not feel me,
Though I feel him,
Undesirable, I guess,
For when my fingers touch him,
He retracts from my caress.

He does not want me,
Though I want him,
Unwanted, you see,
For when I try to hold him,
He seeks for anyone but me.

He does not love me,
Though I love him,
Unlovable, I presume,
For he, to me, is roses,
I to him, are weeds that bloom.

CONCEALING STARS

I trace the constellations,
Star formations in the sky,
This invoked in me, a memory,
Of the one I let slip by.
We were stargazers, dream chasers,
Lovers, you, and I,
Now we are nothing, but a memory,
And with a broken heart, I cry.

I watch the constellations,
Star formations as they glow,
With this memory resurfacing,
I needed to let go.
We were astrologers, night dreamers,
Lovers, but now I know,
That our love was never destined,
And my heart felt every blow.

I reach for the constellations,
Star formations I cannot touch,
But my fingertips conceal the light,
Of the stars I love so much.
We were astrophiles, selenophiles,
Lovers, and as such,
You lost the love you held for me,
When the dark became too much.

WHITE HORSE

I was broken, my heart was aching,
I was fragile and alone,
Seeking for a lover,
For a man to call my own.
I was lonesome, had almost given up,
My heart could take no more,
So many empty promises,
Had hurt me to the core,
And I felt guilty, I self-sabotaged,
From lies, through tears and blame,
Still seeking for prince charming,
On his white horse,

Then you came...

You took my fractured heart,
And you held it in your hand,
As you filled my head with promises,
About our future, you had planned.
Then, you broke me, more than anyone,
And the pain hurt, so much more,
As you let me fall much harder,
Than any man before,

And now I see it...

And my darling, now I know,
That you are not prince charming,
So take your white horse,

And just go.

LACUNA

Who is she?
Do you know?
Have you seen the girl so full of woe?
The one whose eyes are laced with tears?
The girl who fought and failed for years?

No?

Let me show you something, none may know:

She lay to slumber every night,
Beneath the stars, aflame so bright,
And she wished on each for only peace,
To fix her heart back, piece by piece.
She wakes each morn with messy hair,
From tossing, turning, in despair,
Then moments after she awake,
Her heart shall only further break.
Lacuna – this is all she knows,
A hollowness to never close,
Inside a heart, once full and pure,
Now broken, from all she endure.
She lay to slumber every night,
Resolved to win the war she fights,
And beyond her sorrow, tears, and pain,
She fights until the dragons slain,
And there will someday come a day,
She shall wake up healed –

Just not today.

INVISIBLE

I'm invisible, I know this,

None but her can lock your gaze,

Vacant stares are all you give me,

I tried hard, so many ways.

So many times I've tried and failed,

I longed to just be seen,

But I always stayed invisible,

Longing that your gaze, be divisible,

Even though, I know, I'll always, stay, unseen.

HE IS NOT YOU

He is not you, he never was,
He could never take your place,
He longs for me, he aches to be,
The reason, for the smile upon my face.

He is not you, he never was,
He holds me in embrace,
He comforts me, he hopes to see,
My thoughts of you efface.

He is not you, he never was,
He yearns to be my king,
He pines for me, he asks that we,
Be both bound by a ring.

He is not you, he never was,
He has they grayest eyes,
He looks at me, he longs to see,
My own green eyes reprise.

He is not you, he never was,
He never could be you,
He healed my scars beneath the stars,
And he swears his love is true.

But,

He is not you!

I WAS NEVER YOURS

I was never yours, not really,
Though I longed that you be mine,
And I waited with such bated breath,
In the hope we could align.
But the sands of time passed slowly,
And this hope turned to regret,
You were the only one I thought about,
I was unable to forget,
Your deep grey eyes, and piercing gaze,
The fire you sparked, I watched it blaze,
And yet,
As I watched you with that cigarette,
In between each puff you'd pause,
And look, not at, but through me,
As though I was not yours,
As though I was not standing here,
The girl who begged in tears,
The one whose waited patiently,
Heartbreakingly, for years.
You treat me like a puppet,
That was rigged up to a string,
That you had woven round your fingers,
And you caused much suffering,
But the one thing that I see now,
The thing that most endures,
Is that you never really loved me,
And that I was never yours.

TIME

I wish that we could rewind time,

Wish that time could pause,

I wish that we could travel back,

So I could tell you, I am yours.

How I long to travel back, to,

When we both first met,

Each memory I reminisce,

Consumes me with regret.

Our love was pure – unfiltered –

Unique, you owned my heart, but I,

Let time slip away so much, that we,

Drift so far apart.

Rewinding time would give me,

Every chance to change our fate,

We would have been together, and,

I would not make you wait.

Now I know the pain of heartbreak,

Darling I loved you, I still do, but,

Time cannot be rewound, and,

I know that this is true.

Memories last forever, and shall treasure,

Each of you.

DISTANCE

Do you not feel our distance?
How I am close but so far away?
Can you not sense my loneliness?
If you do, why do you stay?

For you do not make me happy,
And I know this to be true,
I wish, I wish, that you'd accept,
That you aren't happy too.

Let me go,
Release me,
So that I may find,
Someone new.

LET ME GO

Let me go,
You know how much this hurts me,
And you've seen the tears I've cried,
You know we are impossible,
For both of us have tried.
We've tried and failed for many years,
To win this war we fight,
But we both know within our hearts,
That you and I aren't right.
I want someone to spill my name,
From lips that ache for mine,
For a man who longs to hold me,
Till I'm lost in his entwine.
I want a man who will bring me flowers,
Because I crossed his mind,
A man who will make love to me,
With a touch that can unwind.
I want a man who dreams of me,
Though I'm laid across his chest.
A man who holds me tenderly,
As his fingertips caress.
Your lips no longer ache for mine,
You don't hold me in your arms,
You never bring me flowers,
And your touch does not disarm.
You never dream about me,
And above all else, I know,
That you are not the one for me,
So I ask, for you to let me go.

'Do you feel Oizy's misery,
Beware her cloak of woe.
For this goddess spreads her poison,
And injects her venom slow'.

APHRODITE

THE STORY OF APHRODITE

Meet Aphrodite, goddess of love,
Of passion and beauty,
Whose body was created,
From the foam upon the sea.

Born off the coast of Cythera,
Her birth had come to be,
When her father was castrated,
And his genitals thrown at sea.

The moment that they mixed with foam,
Aphrodite then arose,
Her beauty was incomparable,
With her naked form exposed.

She was lusted after constantly,
By Gods who craved her touch,
Then was forced by Zeus to marry,
One that she hated very much.

There are stories of this goddess,
Many tales of love affairs,
Adultery surrounds her myth,
Of Gods who made her theirs.

But beneath the tales of passion,
There is one to rise above,
This is the story of Adonis,
And Aphrodite's love.

HEPHAESTUS

Aphrodite sought a lover,
On the island she called home,
And each God upon Olympia,
Desired her for their own.

Zeus had witnessed all the chaos,
As they argued and they fought,
He was angered by her beauty,
And the trouble that it brought.

So he gave her to Hephaestus,
The ugly God of fire,
And she loathed him, but relented,
Though this was not her desire.

She would not offer him fidelity,
Nor appease him in the sheets,
Any chance she had for pleasure,
She would take, and she would cheat.

He resented this, for he felt she,
Should show faithfulness to him,
And after many years of longing,
Hephaestus gave in.

He would catch her in the midst of trysts,
Humiliate her too,
And his jealousy became extreme,
It is what bitterness can do.

ARES

Ares was the God of war,
He could be violent and cruel,
A brutal but a cowardly God,
Who was insatiable in duel.

Renowned for his brute savagery,
And his and Aphrodite's lust,
Ares myth is of love and failure,
Battles and bloodlust.

Every lover that Ares had bed,
Would rarely satisfy,
Only Aphrodite held his lust,
None, but for her, would he die.

So, he spoke of lustful longing,
In the hope she would accede,
Ares wanted her to want him,
For his efforts to succeed.

HIS WORDS

His words penetrate my heart,
They warm me to the core,
When I see his naked body,
My own desires for more.

His voice is sexual and passionate,
His words arouse me so,
I have no control around him,
All restraint, I overthrow.

He speaks about my body,
How he longs that we entwine,
And I ache to give him all of me,
I long that he be mine.

He tells me how I make him feel,
That he longs for me to strip,
So he can kiss and caress my body,
And draw me to him, by my hip.

He whispers words as sweet as wine,
Which intoxicate my mind,
And as he speaks these lustful words,
But for him, I am blind.

WEB OF GOLD THREAD

We were both consumed by passion,

Entwined within my bed,

But I did not know that Helios,

Overlooked us up ahead.

Furious, he told Hephaestus,

Given him the thought, to,

Openly humiliate, to,

Lock us, in our naked state,

Determined we be caught.

Trapped within a golden web,

He flaunt us to the crowd, to be,

Ridiculed, and laughed at,

Each God circled, laughing loud,

Ares, this was both our fault,

Do not act disavowed.

ILLICIT AFFAIR

We were tangled,

You and I,

Ensnared in a web,

That was weaved from a lie,

Still, we tried,

In the darkness to meet,

And in shadows we hide.

We were cloaked,

In deceit,

Enveloped in lies,

Entangled in sheets,

Still, we met,

As Selene cast her spell,

And subdued our regret.

We were blind,

And we fell,

Lost in a lust,

That could never be quelled,

Still, we kissed,

As the darkness concealed,

And secreted our tryst.

We were trapped,

And we yield,

Surrendered to passion,

That both of us wield,

Still, we long,

For time to refrain,

And prove we belong,

In this illicit affair,

That we both know is wrong.

MYRRHA

Myrrha was a mortal girl,
The daughter of a king,
Her story is a treacherous one,
Of envy, jealousy, and sin.

Her father was king Cinyras,
Her mother was Cenchreis,
And Myrrha held such beauty,
That time appeared to freeze.

One day Cenchreis was boasting,
That Myrrha's beauty had outgrown,
Even that of Aphrodite,
She would have stayed silent, had she known.

Once Aphrodite heard these words,
No insult could be worse,
She then sought for retribution,
And inflict a wicked curse.

Myrrha's curse consumed her body,
And it forced her to begin,
An incestuous relationship,
Unknowingly to him.

Her father lay in darkness,
And for several nights, she came,
Till he longed to see the maiden,
The one, with whom, each night, he had lain.

Cinyras was disgusted,
When his lamp revealed her face,
And he tried to kill his daughter,
But she flee her father's chase.

Upon her knees she pleaded,
Begged the Gods to end her pain,
She felt lost, so torn, and broken,
And she cried in such disdain.

Zeus had watched as she unravel,
And took pity on the girl,
As she knelt upon the bank of earth,
Before him and unfurl.

He resolved to end her mortal life,
So Aphrodite's curse would wane,
Not through death, but transformation,
Only this could end her pain.

She was scared, her fears merged with regret,
Albeit, not her fault,
As Zeus acceded to her plea,
And retrieved his thunderbolt.

In that moment, Myrrha's mortal form,
Altered and transpose,
And in the place where she once sat,
A myrrh tree then arose.

Although the curse appeared concluded,
And her impulsion had subside,
None knew the repercussion,
Of the curse, the myrrh tree hide.

ADONIS

The myrrh tree of Myrrha, appeared from the ground,
Its aromatic exuding are her tears which abound.

But this tree holds a secret, none could have believed,
For inside of its trunk, grew the child she conceived.

Her child, born of incest, was fated to grow,
With a beauty not seen before, incomparably so.

A boar then spontaneously made an impact,
And in a matter of seconds, the myrrh tree trunk cracked.

Out came the baby, the myrrh tree expel,
As Aphrodite came walking, right by where he fell.

Aphrodite then named him Adonis, for he,
Was bequeathed, much like her, with the gift of beauty.

She had happened upon him, this newborn, alone,
And resolved she should keep him, only when he had grown.

So she gathered the baby, held him close to her breast,
And sought the solution, to hide him in a chest.

Aphrodite would then ask Persephone to hide,
The chest without knowing, the child was inside.

Then years would go by, and the child would be grown,
And she would take back the chest, and the man that she own.

PERSEPHONE

I have a chest, a trunk of gold,
It is one close to my heart,
Inside there lay the thing it hold,
This thing and I must part.

I ask it stays unopened,
That it does not see the light,
Till the day comes when its opened,
Only when the time is right.

This trunk contains an infant boy,
Born from my wicked curse,
But secretly I must employ,
Persephone as his nurse.

He shall grow into a handsome man,
And his beauty shall ensnare,
But he is mine, it is my plan,
Once he is grown, I shall be there.

I did not want Persephone,
To see Adonis lay,
Inside the chest she keeps for me,
For I know she will betray.

But he is safe here, in the underworld,
No harm this child shall bare,
Whilst in this chest of gold, he is furled,
And is safe within its care.

THE REFUSAL

'You shall not take him from me,
Adonis is my own,
I took him in, I guarded him,
I have watched as he has grown.
His place is in the underworld,
Beside me sits his throne,
You shall not take him from me,
I am all that he has known.
Aphrodite, you must leave now,
Through the gates you shall walk alone,
I refuse to give him back to you,
I shall not live life lone.'

'Persephone, he is not yours,
Adonis is my own,
You took him in, you guarded him,
Temporarily, till grown.
His place is not the underworld,
He has no seat, nor throne,
You shall not keep him from me,
Though you are all that he has known.
Persephone, I shall leave now,
But shall not walk through gates alone,
I shall get Adonis back from you,
I shall not live life lone.'

The goddesses had argued,
And neither would atone,
So they took Adonis up to Zeus,
So he may decide his home.

ZEUS'S VERDICT

Persephone stood to his left,
Aphrodite to his right,
As Zeus could only focus,
On the mortal in his sight.

Persephone then argued,
That Adonis should be hers,
She had raised him from an infant,
She was who the man prefers.

Aphrodite counteracted,
She declared him as her own,
She had only asked Persephone,
To guard him till he's grown.

Zeus reflected on both answers,
Listened closely to their pleas,
He was torn to make a choice,
For only one he could appease.

Zeus declared his final ruling,
And Adonis would now be,
With Aphrodite for four months,
And four with Persephone.

The remaining four months of the year,
Adonis could decide,
To spend it with Persephone,
Or be by Aphrodite's side.

THE MAGICAL GIRDLE OF APHRODITE

The magical girdle of Aphrodite,

Holds the power of lust and sex,

Every man to see it, becomes,

Monopolised by its hex.

Aphrodite uses this,

Girdle to allure,

It holds the power to,

Captivate, entice,

Appease and more.

Lust and sex are imminent, her

Girdle makes it so,

Inner thoughts and fantasies,

Resurface when it shows.

Dangerous, for those who,

Lust, for the goddess in this belt,

Each man shall fall, unknowingly,

Out wittingly, to its spell.

From the pages of mythology,

And Aphrodite's tale,

People were seduced by her,

Her girdle never failed.

Resisting her was futile,

Once her girdle was adorned,

Despite the ones who tried and failed,

It would not leave her scorned.

The girdle of Aphrodite, overrules,

Each man be warned.

LOVE STORY

I was a briar rose,
Standing alone,
Entangled as thorns,
All around me had grown.

Then you saw me, and loved me,
Beyond all your pain,
You recognized that,
You and I were the same.

We had both been neglected,
Abandoned and hurt,
But you saw my strength,
As I bloomed from the dirt.

You believed fate a fairytale,
Soulmates were untrue,
But your perception of both,
Came from those who hurt you.

I will love you forever,
And in twenty years and a day,
You will gaze in my eyes,
And in your arms, I will say,

That each star in the night sky,
Aligned up above,
You are my soulmate, it was fate,
And you are worthy of love.

APHRODITE'S WARNING

'My love', spoke Aphrodite,
'Please heed the words I say,
I should not wish you any harm,
But I fear it comes your way.
My former lover, Ares,
Is a truly jealous man,
And he will seek the death of you,
In any way he can.
Tread careful in the forest,
Avoid boars in your path,
For this could be, a way that he,
Release envious wrath.
I speak these words of warning,
In the hope that you accede,
Adonis, you must listen,
And I need for you to heed,
The words I speak, the things I say,
These are all to keep you safe,
The last thing I would ever want,
Is for you to meet your grave.
So promise me, my lover,
That you shall avoid the boar,
So you can stay beside me,
And I with you, forevermore.

AROUSING HIS JEALOUSY

Persephone went to Ares,
Desperation in her heart,
She longed that Aphrodite,
And Adonis be apart.

She knew Ares was a jealous God,
So she taint his ears with words,
Of his lover, Aphrodite,
Which enflamed him once he heard.

She spoke of how the goddess,
Had fallen for a mortal man,
That no other man had made her feel,
The way Adonis can.

He was furious, and bitter,
Consumed by jealous lust,
He was angry, Aphrodite,
Had betrayed their pledge of trust.

Now, Persephone, could not have known,
What the God, Ares, had planned,
She selfishly believed he would,
Return Adonis to her hand.

But a jealous man shows no restraint,
When revenge is on his mind,
Aphrodite had betrayed him,
Now her lover, he must find.

THE WILD BOAR

He was seeking,
Hurting,
Hunting,
And revenge was on his mind,
He was jealous,
Bitter,
Broken,
And his anger made him blind.

He was creeping,
Tracking,
Tracing,
And he caught him in his sight,
He was hostile,
Sullen,
Somber,
And this death would put things right.

He was watchful,
Patient,
Persistent,
And he prepared to make a strike,
He was appeased,
Eager,
Eased,
As he end his life through bite.

BLOODSTAINED ROSE

Aphrodite felt something was wrong,
A pain came in her chest,
She clutched and pressed upon her breast,
Sat almost naked, barely dressed,
A wave of sadness then impressed,
Upon her mind, which felt depressed,
Though stressed, she remained strong.
She ran into the forest, pained,
She needed to be sure,
That Adonis, the man she adore,
Had not been injured by the boar,
She warned him, it was something more,
A jealous ex to set a score,
He swore, he'd be restrained.
As she ran with naked feet,
Upon a rose of white,
Its thorn had pierced with sharpened bite,
Her blood had stained it, made it blight,
But Aphrodite held much fight,
Until she saw him in her sight,
Her plight ended in defeat.
Her lover now lay motionless,
This was to be his grave,
He had ignored advice she gave,
And taunt the boar, for he felt brave,
The blood on the white rose, engraved,
And in her heart, a hole was staved,
Carved and emotionless.

ANEMONE

She lay across her lovers chest,
And begged for him to wake,
She asked the Fates to bring him back,
There are other lives to take.

As she lay there in the forest,
She awaited their reply,
But she knew it was impossible,
And Adonis had to die.

The forest that became his grave,
Was the same one where they met,
She questioned why he had to die,
And she held him with regret.

She began to cry, from heartache,
As she held his soulless form,
And as her tears merged with his blood,
An anemone was born.

This flower bloomed upon his chest,
Its petals, red as blood,
It symbolized both love and death,
United in one bud.

This anemone was her goodbye,
A farewell to the one,
Who she loved unconditionally,
Eternally, though gone.

LOST LOVER

My eyes are laced with tears,
Full of fear,
They appear,
To be full of pain and sorrow,
From your absence as you leave,
And you left my own heart broken,
Words misspoken,
Some unspoken,
And you left unanswered questions,
As you left me here to grieve.

My broken heart was shattered,
It was tattered,
Nothing mattered,
As you walked into the distance,
And you faded from my view,
With your reasons, undelivered,
I just shivered,
My lips quivered,
Standing outside in a blizzard,
As I said goodbye to you.

My mind of thoughts were racing,
Each unlacing,
I was tracing,
Every memory we had ever made,
To find the one that made you go,
And I played them in slow motion,
Stood here frozen,
In remotion,

Conflicted feelings of devotion,
That enveloped me in woe.

My palms were numb and frosted,
I was exhausted,
Undefrosted,
As I stood out here in winter,
And I tried to wave goodbye,
But my hands were not acceding,
Disbelieving,
You were leaving,
And they knew that I was grieving,
So they both refused to try.

My heart began rejecting,
Redirecting,
And deflecting,
Any blame or guilty feelings,
You had forced me to believe,
For you were the knight I trusted,
Armuor rusted,
Falsely encrusted,
A wolf in sheepskin clothing,
My lost lover who deceived.

ELYSIAN

She said goodbye to her lover,
As he lay upon the earth,
Caressed his face, and kissed his lips,
And told him of his worth.

There could never be another man,
To own her heart, like he,
For she gave him it sometime before,
And did so, willingly.

He was perfect to Aphrodite,
And no other could compare,
The misfortune of his death had brought,
The goddess much despair.

For she loved him, it was special,
Something never felt before,
And she was angry towards Ares,
Who she knew became the boar.

She had tried her best to keep him safe,
And had warned him of the signs,
He had not listened to his lovers words,
Though she told him, many times.

And now he is elysian,
In the Gods own afterlife,
And Aphrodite lost her lover,
And in place of him, came strife.

'Do you see an anemone?
A flower of love and pain?
If you do, then Aphrodite,
Mourns her lover who was slain.'

PERSEPHONE

THE STORY OF PERSEPHONE

Meet Persephone, the goddess,
Of harvest and fertility,
And the queen who rules the underworld,
She was the only dual deity.

Persephone was a maiden,
Who was beautiful and fair,
But was stolen to the underworld,
And became imprisoned there.

Her father, Zeus, is God of sky,
And Demeter is her mother,
Unwillingly, it came to be,
That Hades was her lover.

Also known by the name, 'Kore',
This goddess held much power,
For she held a unique gift,
To transform anything to a flower.

Persephone loved the meadow,
It was like a second home,
Till one visit cost her greatly,
In the seconds she roamed alone.

Her story is so bittersweet,
A tale to break the heart,
One of innocence, and purity,
Stolen at least, in part.

HADES

Hades was God of the underworld,
And also the Greek lord of death,
He dwell below earth, in the fiery abyss,
A place that he rarely had left.

Awe inspiring, but so terrifying,
With the helm of darkness adorned,
He would carry a Bident, his weapon of choice,
And would use it on any who scorned.

Depicted as handsome, but frightening,
Hades invoke a feeling of dread,
His name derives from, 'the unseen one',
An apt title for the lord of the dead.

Ever since he laid eyes on Persephone,
His obsession with her, never ceased,
He would do what he had to, no matter the cost,
To make her the queen of the deceased.

Solemn, and mournful, and angry,
Feared, revered, and dire,
Hades is the brother of Poseidon, and Zeus,
And he dwells below earth, in hellfire.

LIMERENCE

She possessed him, unknowingly,
He had fell for her allure,
And he burned with such intensity,
Ferociously, he roar.

His mind altered, undeniably,
He believed his love returned,
Infatuated by the girl,
For only her, he burned.

He wanted her, unquestionably,
Each night he closed his eyes,
And in his dreams, she would appear,
Each time this would apprise.

She enveloped him, uncontrollably,
And he was haunted by her face,
As he spurned the love of others,
All, but for her, would efface.

His eyes sought for her, understandably,
For she captivate his mind,
He believed the Fates decreed this,
That their threads had been combined.

He desired her, unequivocally,
So obsessively compelled,
To yearn for her, and burn for her,
With a fire to not be quelled.

NARCISSUS

Narcissus was son of Cephissus,
And a nymph, named Liriope,
His beauty, indescribable,
His nature, unjustifiable,
For he was a misanthrope.

Many nymphs had fell for him,
Yet each, Narcissus scorned,
No veil concealed the Gods contempt,
He made no effort to pre-empt,
The disdain his face adorned.

One day whilst he was hunting,
In the woodland near his home,
The nymph, Echo, was walking,
She had heard Narcissus talking,
And desired him for her own.

Revealing herself to him,
She grasped him in embrace,
Narcissus pushed her, callously,
So forcefully, maliciously,
With distaste upon his face.

Echo had been rejected,
A pain she could not bear,
She roamed the woods for many years,
Until she wilted from her tears,
And died from her despair.

Nemesis had been witness,
To the pain Narcissus formed,
The goddess of retribution,
Vowed he shall face persecution,
For this man was unreformed.

She led Narcissus to a pool,
With water crystal clear,
He gaze down with such affection,
Falling for his own reflection,
But to him, this was unclear.

Once he learned it was a mirror,
That this man shall not appear,
His mind was so foreboding,
As he felt his heart corroding,
For the one he loved so dear.

For the longest time he sat there,
Growing weaker by the day,
Till the darkness came surrounding,
He submerged, and he was drowning,
Then a flower bloomed where he lay.

This flower became Narcissus,
A bloom of white and gold,
With a fragrance so narcotic,
And appearance so hypnotic,
It ensnares those who behold.

THE ABDUCTION

The Nysian meadow was beautiful,
Starred with flowers, bright and bold,
And this meadow captivated,
As the sun bathed it in gold.

There were roses, and crocus,
Violet, and larkspur,
Orchid, iris, aster,
And they bloomed because of her.

Persephone adored this meadow,
With its scent of sweet perfume,
In every footprint she impressed,
Another flower would bloom.

The Oceanids accompanied her,
Each visit that she made,
These ocean nymphs protected her,
To ensure she never strayed.

A day had come, none could foretell,
Though written by the Fates,
That would leave the Oceanids aggrieved,
Alone, in desperate straits.

The goddess saw a flower,
Unlike any she had seen,
It was gold, and white, and sprang upright,
So hypnotically serene.

She walked to it entrancingly,
Unaware she walked alone,
She then reached out for the flower,
That had bloomed, remote, and lone.

Its scent was so narcotic,
And it took hold of her mind,
From the moment she beheld it,
To all, but for it, she was blind.

The nymphs were dancing in the meadow,
Uprooting flowers from the ground,
Not one had seen Persephone,
Withdraw, without a sound.

As her fingers trace the Narcissus,
The earth shook and unfold,
And from the ground, Hades upbound,
In his chariot of gold.

Persephone cried out in fear,
And it echoed through the air,
The Oceanids had heard her cry,
But could not find her anywhere.

The God then gripped her by her arm,
And forced her by his side,
As he descended to the underworld,
Hades and his bride.

THE FIELDS OF THE UNDERWORLD:

The fields of punishment:

In the deepest depths of the underworld,
Are the fields of punishment,
A dungeon of torture and suffering,
Where all sinful souls are sent.
This deep abyss is torturous,
And its torment shall not end.
Each punishment the judges choose,
Are unique to those condemned.
The three judges choose their ruling,
And the souls they force to dwell,
In this place, also named Tartarus,
Are exposed to living hell.

The fields of mourning:

In the 'Aeneid', in the underworld,
The mourning fields await,
A place of woe, and sorrow,
Full of sadness, and heartbreak.
This realm within the underworld,
Is a place that holds much pain,
As the souls the judges send here,
Forever, mourn their lover, unattained.
The three judges choose their ruling,
And the souls to waste their life,
Pursuing unrequited love,
Are sentenced to this place of strife.

The Asphodel meadows:

In a realm within the underworld,
Sits the Asphodel meadows,
A place that held indifferent souls,
Crime free, but not heroes.
A place for neutral mortals,
Where their souls shall stay lifelong,
Any soul the judges send here,
Did, in the other three, not belong.
The three judges choose their ruling,
And if a soul was ordinary,
They would be sentenced to this realm,
That mirrors life, eternally.

The Elysian fields:

In a beautiful realm of the underworld,
There sits the Elysian fields,
Awe inspiring, divine, peaceful, and fine,
Where both heroes and Gods are concealed.
Also known as Elysium,
This tranquil realm pertain,
Any soul the judges send here,
Shall be free from affliction and pain.
The three judges choose their ruling,
And if a soul was heroic, or pure,
They were welcomed to Elysium,
Labour free, forevermore.

THREE JUDGES OF THE DEAD

Three judges sit debating,
Where each mortal soul reside,
As they judge the deeds of those deceased,
Before the three decide.

These three govern the underworld,
And each one invoke dread,
Let me introduce them to you,
Meet the judges of the dead.

Aeacus:

Aeacus was a former king, of a Saronic isle in Greece.
Upon his death, he became a judge, and guardian of the keys.
He was said to be a pious ruler, sanctimonious, but fair,
Who would decide the fate of European souls, sent there.

Rhadamanthus:

Rhadamanthus was a former king, of a Greek island, called Crete.
Upon his death, he became a judge, with Elysium's throne, his seat.
He was said to be inflexible, indomitable, but wise,
Who would decide the fate of Eastern souls, and where each lies.

Minos:

Minos was a former king, and Rhadamanthus was his kin.
Upon his death, he became a judge, with final votes being left to him.
He was said to be a cruel tyrant, manipulative, but brave,
If his brothers' judgment both conflict, his own, would, their choice, waive.

POMEGRANATE SEED

It seduced me,
Seductively,
With its luster,
As it drips,
So enticingly,
It longed to be,
Impressed, within my lips.

It entranced me,
Captivatingly,
This blood red,
Lacquered pip,
So cunningly,
It wished for me,
To take one bite, one nip.

It possessed me,
Hauntingly,
Longed to be,
Within my grip,
So uncontrollably,
It craved to see,
My tongue lick it, with the tip.

It deceived me,
Deceptively,
All it took,
Was just one sip,
So forcefully,
Trapped eternally,
As decreed by Hades script.

SIX MONTHS

Hades tricked her, had deceived her,
Kept her captive far below,
He had tempted her, deceptively,
But withheld what she should know.

He had offered her a taste of fruit,
A pomegranate seed,
But this food was of the underworld,
Those to taste it, could not be freed.

Persephone had swallowed six,
Which meant that she would spend,
Six months within the underworld,
Each year, till her life end.

Persephone surrendered,
She relent to Hades law,
It would not serve a purpose,
Only hurt the goddess more.

She was bound by rules of Hades,
It was meaningless to fight,
Though she longed to hold her mother,
And she ached to see the light.

So it was written that Persephone,
Was trapped beneath the ground,
Appointed queen of death by Hades,
And, for six months, stay unfound.

DEPRESSION IS

An overwhelming sadness,
A shadow in your mind,
It is late night tears, and morning fears,
It is cruel, and never kind.

It is saying no to invites,
Even though you long to go,
It is unwashed hair, from lack of care,
For your self-esteem is low.

It is crying in the shower,
As your water blends with tears,
It is a burden that you carry,
And have done so, many years.

It is lonesome, and it isolates,
But I swear you are not alone,
I see the pain within your eyes,
Please do not face this on your own.

There is a light, one day you will it,
And my darling, it is so bright,
Even though it seems impossible,
You are strong, you will be alright.

DEMETER

Demeter was the goddess,
Of the fruitfulness of earth,
Persephone was her daughter,
And she loved her child since birth.

A day came when she heard her scream,
From far across the land,
Demeter raced across the planes,
To see what was at hand.

When she landed in the forest,
Where her flower basket lay,
She was searching, seeking, desperately,
To find who took her child away.

Demeter panicked, stopping Gods,
And mortals, any in her path,
Asking who had took Persephone,
But those who knew, feared Hades wrath.

They were silent, and for nine days,
Demeter searched all land and sky,
On the morning of the tenth day,
Hecate had heard her cry.

She consoled the grieving mother,
And agreed to aid her plight,
Then they both appealed to Helios,
The all-seeing God of light.

He revealed to them, the tragic tale,
How Hades stole the girl,
How he abducted sweet Persephone,
And dragged her to the underworld.

In the absence of Persephone,
Demeter vowed that she,
Would ensure that earth should suffer,
Till her daughter was set free.

Zeus could see the desperate mortals,
Hear them beg from starving mouths,
As Demeter failed the harvest,
So strong willed to keep her vows.

Zeus ordered that her daughter,
Be returned, so earth may see,
A harvest, no more famine,
And fruit to bloom from every tree.

But Hades tricked Persephone,
He was cruel, intentions clear,
And he forced the goddess, callously,
To return for six months every year.

KALOPSIA

She gaze at him,
She trace his chest,
She whispered out his name.
She longed to feel him deep within,
She hoped he felt the same.
She kissed his lips,
She touched his face,
She whispered words of trust.
She listened to the words he spoke,
She looked at him through lust.
She called his name,
She held him close,
She saw his naked build.
She desired for their rhythmic flow,
She knew he would be skilled.
She ached for him,
She believed within,
She felt ataraxia,
She did not see the reality,
She suffered from kalopsia.

PETRICHOR

The word 'Petra',
Means stone,
And ichor,
Is the ethereal blood,
That flows,
Through the bones,
Of the Gods,
That withstood.
Petrichor,
Is the smell after rain,
After droughts, after floods.

It is the scent,
In the air,
When the rain has submitted,
And poured,
As the oils,
From the plants.
Are released,
As the moisture absorbs.
She had sworn,
To ensure,
No rain pours, evermore.

But her child,
Was returned,
So, she let the rain pour,
And it fell,
Hungry mouths,
Were all fed,
She retracted the drought,
She now quells.
Earth restores,
As it pours,
They adore, petrichor.

WINTER

She grieves for you, Persephone,
And her isolation shows,
For six months of each passing year,
The earth shall remain froze,
For the snow blanket upon the earth,
Secretes your mothers woes,
And none, but you, shall melt the ice,
Around her heart, that grows.

She misses you, Persephone,
And the winter shows her pain,
For six months of each passing year,
The life on earth, shall wane,
For the harshness of the bitter air,
Reflects your mothers own disdain,
And her warmth and love shall dissipate,
Until you return again.

She cries for you, Persephone,
And her pain is not disguised,
For six months of each passing year,
The sun shall never rise,
For the earth does not deserve this gift,
Your mother had surmised,
And her sadness shows through winter,
Till you stand before her eyes.

SPRING

She holds you close, Persephone,
And her heart is so elate,
For six months of each passing year,
The earth shall celebrate,
For the harvest shall be plentiful,
And your mother shall not abate,
Her boundless, endless, infiniteness,
Promise, earth shall now create.

She smiles for you, Persephone,
And the spring depicts her glow,
For six months of each passing year,
The life on earth shall grow,
For the warmth of sun, shall overrun,
As your mothers gift, bestow,
And her happiness at your return,
Shall, through the springtime, show.

She loves you, Persephone,
And her mind is calm, and free,
For six months of each passing year,
The sun shall shine freely,
For the earth deserves the joy she feels,
Now your mother is carefree,
And her love for you, comes shining through,
At your return, Persephone.

ABIENCE

Abience – withdrawal –
She knew she had to leave,
Every word he ever told her,
Was a lie that she believed.

He would cloak her in false promise,
Whilst she gaze into his eyes,
But this opia, deceived her,
And she listened to his lies.

She had longed to find her soulmate,
And believed this was achieved,
She spoke openly, and honestly,
But he betrayed her and deceived.

There were moments, she was happy,
But those days were far and few,
As lies would slip between his lips,
Concealing what was true.

The thing most unforgivable,
Far beyond her broken heart,
Was that he could see that she was weak,
And he let her fall apart.

But a day came, and with it, strength,
An emotion never known,
Abience – withdrawal –
And she left him all alone.

WHITE STARGAZER LILY

White stargazer lilies represent Persephone,

Her nature is alike this flower of love, and purity.

It is precious, and symbolic,

They represent virginity,

Every petal blooms in perfect grace,

Similar to Persephone.

The name derives from 'leirion',

A Greek word, they assigned,

Romantically, to fit this flower,

Growing, perfectly designed.

A goddess of such modesty,

Zealously astute,

Eternally, the white lily,

Reaffirms her kindred roots.

Lilies mirror life and death,

It has no single undertone,

Like Persephone, with euphony,

You can designate your own.

DULCET

Her dulcet voice, lulled him,
And it eased his weary mind,
He would listen, so intently,
As her voice made him unwind.
She would hold him close, in her embrace,
As words spilled from her lips,
Words of comfort, lust, and longing,
From her own handwritten scripts.
As she read the words aloud to him,
In her unique and dulcet tone,
He found that he was falling,
Wishing she could be his own.

His dulcet voice, lulled her,
And impressed within her mind,
She would listen, so intently,
As his voice made her unwind.
He would hold her close, in his embrace,
As words poured from his lips,
Words of praise, of love, of passion,
About her own handwritten scripts.
As he spoke these words to her,
In his unique and dulcet tone,
She found that she was falling,
Wishing he could be her own.

GOODBYES ARE NEVER EASY

Goodbyes are never easy,

Once they leave, your heart shall break,

Our existence is not permanent,

Death shall come and he shall take.

Broken hearts are a recurrent theme,

You just cannot evade,

Everyone must lose someone they love,

Souls of those you love, shall fade.

A broken heart, shall one day heal,

Repair itself through time,

Every memory you made,

Never shall decline.

Even though you say goodbye,

Vocally, or in thought,

Every photograph, and memory, shall,

Reminisce the bliss they brought.

Even though you said goodbye,

And you feel like you are alone,

Souls become something beautiful,

You have a guardian angel of your own.

PERSEPHONE AND HADES

His mind fixed with obsession,
For possession,
With aggression,
Resolute that he should have her,
As wife and queen of the dead,
But this place was cold and daunting,
It was taunting, and was haunting,
It was not of her desire,
To dwell in this abyss of dread.

Her mind fixed with depression,
Non-aggression,
And oppression,
As Hades had abducted her,
And imprisoned her below,
But this place was mortifying,
Terrifying, horrifying,
It was dark and sun denying,
Where no flowers bloom and grow.

Their minds fixed on each other,
As a lover,
They discover,
That their bond was growing stronger,
As her love for him had formed,
And this place that she once feared,
She now revered, and endeared,
As she share his bed, and wore his crown,
Upon her head, adorned.

'Do you hear a maiden's cry?
Or feel the winter frost?
Then Persephone is in the underworld,
Forbidden fruit came with a cost.'

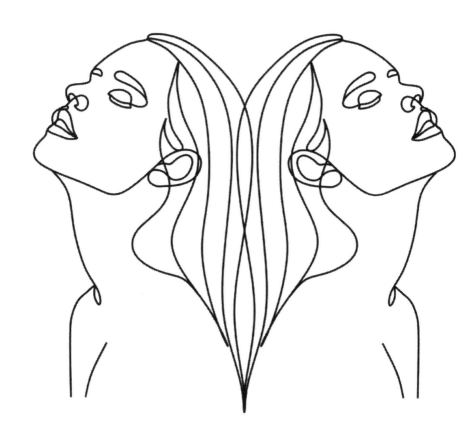

THE FATES

THE STORY OF THE FATES

Meet Clotho, Lachesis, and Atropos,
The goddesses of fate,
The apportioners of mortal life,
Each life, these three dictate.

The past, present, and future,
Are embodied in these three,
As each create, allot, then end,
Each mortals destiny.

It is said, within the first three days,
Of every babies birth,
The Fates appear, and each decide,
Their lifespan on the earth.

They were, all three, the daughters,
Of the God of sky, named Zeus,
And their mother was called Themis,
Goddess of justice, wisdom, truth.

The fates were once called Moirai,
For they apportion life to all,
But they also take away this gift,
And make both Gods and mortals fall.

Be warned, for when it comes to fate,
And how all lives are played,
That Clotho, Lachesis, and Atropos,
Could not, by none, be swayed.

CLOTHO

Clotho was the youngest fate,
Of the sisters, three,
She spun the thread of human life,
The thread of destiny.

Her role throughout mythology,
Is vital above all,
For she could grant the power of life,
Or have Gods and mortals fall.

She would spin the thread within her hands,
And choices would be made,
The thread controlled the fate of all,
And how their lives were played.

There is a tale been told through time,
Of Clotho's thread and pen,
How she forced Aphrodite,
To have sex with other men.

But her choice, once made, was final,
Twined in the thread that she create,
No mortal being, or ancient God,
Could deviate from fate.

LACHESIS

Lachesis was the middle fate,
Of the sisters, three,
She measured out the thread of life,
That controlled all destiny.

She was known as the apportioner,
And would measure with her rod,
A length of thread that Clotho spun,
For the lifespan of each God.

Lachesis wore mainly white,
And her name instilled such fear,
For she would choose the length of time,
A person had, once here.

At the birth of every child,
She would visit in three days,
And make her choice, about their fate,
How the lives of each one plays.

But her choice, once made, was final,
And the length that she would give,
Would predetermine just how long,
Each God and mortal live.

ATROPOS

Atropos was the eldest fate,
Of the sisters, three,
She would cut the thread of life,
To end ones destiny.

Where Clotho spun the thread of life,
And Lachesis gave time,
Atropos would bring their end,
By severing their twine.

She was known as the unalterable,
And mythology will say,
That she is the inflexible one,
No God or man could sway.

Atropos would choose the way,
A life would come to end,
Feared and revered, as all adhered,
To the rulings that she penned.

But her choice, once made, was final,
And once the thread was snipped,
A God or mortals life would end,
As destined by her script.

GOLDEN THREAD

Golden thread connects us,

Overlocking twine,

Lachesis had measured and,

Determined we entwine.

Every path, each step we took,

No matter where it lead,

Turned out to be predestiny,

Her book of life would read.

Ruled by fate, it binds us,

Each fibre that she make,

Aligns and twines our golden skeins,

Designed to never break.

YOU

You traced stars around my scars,
And they flickered,
Golden,
Glittered,
And I love you for it.

You placed stardust in my eyes,
And they shimmered,
Sparkled,
Glimmered,
And I am grateful for it.

You chased stars for me to have one,
And they were shooting,
Fast,
Rerouting,
And I appreciate you for it.

You faced sleepless nights to stargaze,
And they glistened,
Flit,
Unconditioned,
And I will never forget you for it.

And…I will always love you!

WRITTEN IN THE STARS

We were written in the stars,

Read them, can you see?

Inside the constellations,

There are the names of you and me.

They are glittered, and they sparkle,

Every night they grace the sky,

No one but us can see them, they are,

Invisible, way up high.

Now do you see them? As they glisten,

They shall only show what's true,

How many can you count?

Each spell out the name of you.

So our names are penned in starlight,

They are written out in gold,

And the love that we both hold,

Resonates, illuminates, emanates, we are,

Soulmates, scripted by the Fates.

PROPHETIC DEITIES

Their eyes were closed, and darkness circled,
Storm clouds overhead,
The sisters held the thread of life,
For the one soon to be dead.

They had been there, three days from his birth,
So many years before,
And predestined that his life would end,
At the age of fifty-four.

At fifty-four, they pulled his thread,
A thread Clotho had weaved,
That Lachesis had measured,
And now Atropos would cleave.

He had begged them, he had pleaded hard,
Their minds could not be swayed,
So Atropos caressed his thread,
Until it's fibres frayed.

He grew weaker, still he pleaded,
Though he knew they would not bend,
The sisters, three, had all agreed,
His life come to its end.

The time had come, his thread was weak,
He was silent, wracked with strife,
As the eldest fate, retrieved her shears,
And cut his thread of life.

PUPPET

I gave you my heart,
But the thing I didn't realise,
Is that by giving you my heart,
I gave you the chance to break it.
Oh, you did!
You filled my head with empty promises,
That you couldn't keep,
Filled my head with visions,
You knew that I would never see.
You blinded me,
With false love,
Fake love.
I was a puppet on your string,
And you pulled me, and pushed me,
Like a toy, and I let you,
But not anymore,
I see the truth now,
And this epiphany,
Hurts me more than you ever could.
This is a letter to you,
From the broken pieces of a heart,
That you shattered and stole,
But it will heal,
I will find real love,
Someone that deserves my smile,
And all the while,
You will watch in the background,
And one day,
However long that may be,
You will realise you lost,
The best thing that you had,
You lost me.

IVY

My heart was a garden,
Long overgrown,
From seeds men had planted,
With promises, sown.

And they grew with intensity,
Too much, I suppose,
Abandoned, neglected,
Each one overgrows.

Then you came and planted,
Your ivy from seed,
You enveloped my heart,
And concealed every weed.

Every leaf was a promise,
you swore you would keep,
As you covered my heart,
And your roots buried deep.

It is true what they say,
About soulmates and fate,
For you tended my garden,
Repairing its state.

And my heart is now cloaked,
In the ivy of you,
It is beautifully strong,
A magnificent view.

I LOVE YOU

You,
Touched me,
Caressed me,
Held me in embrace,
No other,
Had kissed me,
Whilst holding my face.

You,
Held me,
Enveloped me,
I felt safe in your arms,
No lover,
Before,
Had the power to disarm.

You,
Loved me,
You wanted me,
I wanted you too,
No other,
Has ever,
Made me feel how you do.

I love you.

WHAT IS LOVE?

I spoke a while, of many things,
With this stranger I had met,
He'd been hurt by all that love could bring,
And we spoke for hours, but yet.

He asked me what I thought of love,
What does it really mean?
How do you know you've met your soulmate?
Can love be felt? Or touched? or seen?

And I paused, just for a little while,
I longed to make him see,
That though he had been hurt before,
This is what love means, well, to me.

You long to grasp this person,
To hold them in embrace,
And you feel like you've both met before,
In a different time and place.

You long to gift them roses,
For they have crossed your mind all day,
And when you speak, they listen,
But take in each word you say.

And as you lay in bed each night,
As you both lay entwined,
You feel like fate had meant for this,
That your love had been designed.

SOULMATE

You and I were fated,
It was like the universe had planned,
That after many years of searching,
My hand would find your hand.

With you, I share a deep connection,
One that cannot be described,
And in the chambers of my heart,
Only your name is inscribed.

You plant a seed of ivy,
And I was enveloped in your vine,
Every kiss, and word, and longing look,
Made sure our hearts align.

And I love you, in the truest form,
That I have ever known,
I'm so grateful to the universe,
For making you my own.

My love for you is boundless,
It is infinite and true,
And I know that soul mates do exist,
For I found my own,

In you.

CONSTELLATION

You are a constellation of stars,
In the dark of my mind,
In my times of despair,
You are there to remind,
That though I feel lost,
There is always a light,
Even though it is hard,
You remain shining bright,
Just for me,
And I love you for that.

PAST PRESENT FUTURE

The Past:

You have been here, and experienced this,
You cannot change what once has passed,
Mistakes, missteps, and memories,
Are embedded in your past.
Once you have been through it,
One thing shall remain true,
That all your past experiences,
Are what truly makes you, you.

The Present:

You are here now, going through this,
You can change each path you take,
Dreams, desires, and destiny,
Stand before you, they await.
Once you have made your choices,
Based on where you have been before,
New chapters will unfold for you,
And fate will change the score.

The Future:

You are not here yet, but it will come,
You have no clue what this could be,
Unwritten, unseen, and unknowing,
Is your future, yet to see.
Once it comes, you shall reflect,
On where you once have stood,
The future is what you make it,
So every chapter, make them good.

STARGAZING

Stargaze with me darling,
Let us lay beneath their light,
And here upon this bank of earth,
I shall tell you all about your worth,
As we watch the stars ignite.

I long to see a shooting star,
With your fingers locked in mine,
Neither speak, but we both listen,
As it soars above and glistens,
Tearing, beautifully divine.

Count the stars, my lover,
There are so many to see,
Their illuminated, golden hue,
Are works of art, I watch with you,
As you lay here beside me.

Choose a star, and make a wish,
As you slowly close your eyes,
Then watch the star you wished upon,
Dim its light, till it has gone,
The sight will mesmerize.

Then fall asleep, my darling,
Beneath this blanket, full of stars,
Wrapped in my arms,
You are safe from harm,
Let the starlight heal your scars.

CARDIGAN

I want you to be my cardigan,
To caress and feel my skin,
To warm me on the coldest nights,
To comfort me within.
To hold my body softly,
To bask me in your scent,
To be wrapped around my naked breasts,
To cloak me and augment.
To nuzzle me in softness,
To ease and wipe my tears,
To be faithful and consistent,
To not change throughout the years.
To always be my favourite,
To forever be in view,
To eternally be there for me,
To not change,
To just be you.

EVERMORE

Every promise that I give you,

Vision I make you see,

Each spoken word, each kiss, each look,

Reinforce your love for me.

My heart belongs to only you,

Our love is sealed by fate,

Remember that forever, and,

Eternally, I shall wait.

This is my promise to you,
To the man I so adore,
I will love you forever,
And for always, evermore.

GRANDAD

I want to tell you all the sweetest tale,
Told from the kindest man,
It is the story of my Grandad,
And how he met my Nan.

It is a story of coincidence,
But my favourite, for it is pure,
My grandad said he had never fell,
As hard as that before.

They both had a chance meeting,
In a place that neither should have been,
And she was the most beautiful,
Girl he had ever seen.

Her laugh, her eyes, her hair of red,
All captivate him so,
And ever since the night they met,
His love for her would grow.

He loved her, like no other could,
And he offered the best life,
The proudest memory that he has,
Was when she became his wife.

And when I think about it, really,
About their coincidental tryst,
If fate had not aid them to meet,
Then I, would not, exist.

BEAUTY FROM WITHIN

There is a thing so precious,
Beneath a person's skin,
Beyond what other eyes can see,
It is beauty from within.

And it dazzles with intensity,
Shines brighter than the sun,
It is beautiful, and priceless,
And it emanates and stuns.

It is unique to each person,
But my darling, how it shines,
If you gaze beyond the obvious,
And you read between the lines.

For those who choose to cast their gaze,
Beyond what you see clear,
You shall see the inner beauty,
Of the person standing here.

And with compassion and civility,
With virtue and with love,
You can see the beauty held within,
And shall see it always,

Thereof.

'Do you feel the thread of fate?
That binds your mortal form,
Then the three Fates hold it in their hands,
And tease the strands till worn.'

ASTERIA

THE STORY OF ASTERIA

Meet Asteria, 'the starry one',
Who graces with her light,
As the goddess of each falling star,
She dazzles in the night.

Her father's name was Coeus,
A Titan God of mind,
And her mother's name was Phoebe,
A goddess, wise and kind.

She had one sister, Leto,
Who, in Zeus, had lit a fire,
She gave birth to his children,
Which inflamed the God's wife's ire.

Asteria soon fell in love,
With Perses, God of war,
And they shared a daughter, Hecate,
A child they both adore.

When Perses was imprisoned,
By the thunder Gods command,
Zeus tried to bed Asteria,
Who fled, evading his demand.

So, Asteria would risk her life,
To avoid the lust of Zeus,
She would never be duplicitous,
She could never be seduced.

PERSES

Clotho spun the thread of life,
And bound ours tightly so,
That you and I were fated,
With a love the Fates bestow.

Though you are a God of war,
No matter what you do,
Our love was etched by all three fates,
Who bound my thread to you.

They crossed our paths together,
And they watched our flame ignite,
You were the only Titan God,
To set my heart alight.

My love for you is infinite,
Like the stars from which I am named,
It is pure, sincere, and ethereal,
And could never be explained.

Perses, you shall always be,
My consort, lover, friend,
No other man could fill the void,
If your thread comes to its end.

So, forever I shall love you,
And none shall take your place,
For you shall be the only man,
To hold me in embrace.

PATTERN OF STARS

Our kiss formed,
A constellation above,
In starlight, the night sky,
Secreted our love,
And only our eyes,
Were left able to view,
The pattern of stars,
That connect me to you.
It was beautiful,
The scene that unfold,
The stars cloaked our secrets,
In dazzling gold,
As they flickered,
And danced like a flame,
Every wish I made on them,
Pertained to your name,
It was magic,
And each word I impart,
Would be spoken, transfixed,
With such hope in my heart,
I was longing,
For the stars to align,
To answer my wish,
That you could be mine,
Not in secrecy,
But beyond darkened night,
No more stolen kisses,
We could kiss in the light,
For eternity,
And I hope they accede,
For the stars know the truth,
And in fate I believe.

HECATE

Asteria held her daughter,
Swaddled, in embrace,
She gaze upon her little girl,
And kissed her newborn face.

Her little eyes of emerald, green,
Were gazing back in awe,
As her mother spoke with gentle voice,
Of the future she foresaw:

'You shall be so powerful,
I foresee something great,
No harm shall come upon you,
I see magic in your fate.

You see, my darling Hecate,
Your destiny is clear,
Your name shall send a tremor,
And the world shall tread in fear.

You shall dwell in realms of necromancy,
And your flames shall guide the way,
For mortals whose lips spill your name,
As their souls are pulled away.

You shall walk the realms of darkness,
Where your name shall be revered,
For you, my darling Hecate,
Shall be worshipped, laud and feared.

You shall live a life of solitude,
But do not let this dismay,
For two hounds shall offer company,
Both are loyal and shall obey.

You shall not suffer my fate,
The one that still portend,
No God, nor man, shall make you flee,
For your powers shall defend.

Your name derives from Hekatos,
(A worker from afar)
I named you this to coincide,
With mine, named from a star.

You are a goddess, daughter,
Witchcraft courses through your veins,
A sorceress of potency,
And a titaness who reigns'.

Asteria then lulled her child,
Beneath a starlit night,
As both of them were showered,
In its hue of golden light.

Hecate then drift to sleep,
In a state of tranquil rest,
As her mother held the future queen,
Of witchcraft to her breast.

LETTER TO ZEUS

Your eyes ablaze with fire,
Pure desire, I inspire,
Lustful thoughts within your mind,
From my beauty which allures,
But your lust was unrequited,
Uninvited, unignited,
You could never freely have me,
For my body is not yours.

Your heart craved domination,
Exploitation, and invasion,
Of my body and my freedom,
Something you could not attain,
But your quest shall not be fruitful,
Though inscrutable, and brutal,
I should rather die a thousand deaths,
And with each, suffer pain.

Your mind fixed with obsession,
Forced oppression for transgression,
Resolute that you should have me,
In your chamber and your bed,
But your chase was cruel and callous,
Phallus throbbing, fuelled with malice,
Meaning one of us, or both of us,
Would surely end up dead.

QUAIL

I look to the skies, seeing advice,
From stars as they glisten and glow,
Zeus's obsession for my body's possession,
Gave me no choice, I had to go.

I sought for my ancestors' answers,
That came in a shower of gold,
I shall transform myself to a creature,
Long enough for his quest to turn cold.

I was quailed by his boundless advances,
And repelled by this God I distrust,
I transformed to a quail, who could soar and prevail,
To evade his duplicitous lust.

I had given up hope in Olympia,
Knowing that I could never go home,
I knew that he would not surrender,
His resolve was as strong as my own.

But Zeus was determined to have me,
And would scour earth and sky, day, and night,
So, he transformed himself to an eagle,
A bird with strong wings, meant for flight.

Now Zeus was an eagle, the hunter,
And I, as a quail, was his prey,
I shall do what I have to, to lose him,
And shall keep his constrainment at bay.

COLLIDE

Parallel, the sea and sky,
Paradoxical, this night,
I am tired, so tired of running,
And I ache, too much, for flight.

The sky grieves me in silence,
As the stars foretell my fate,
The sea crashes with ferocity,
For its murky depths await.

Your chase is unrelenting,
But it shall conclude this night,
You believe that with persistence,
You can suffocate my fight.

So, I cast my gaze upon the sea,
And with each crashing wave,
I knew that I could not turn back,
The sea shall be my grave.

A single tear rolls down my cheek,
But this is not for you,
I cry because I shall be free,
From all you put me through.

And I plummet, with my eyes closed,
My last act of deride,
As my body hits the stormy sea,
I smile as we collide.

POSEIDON

My body submerged beneath a wave,
That pulled me to its seabed grave.
A moon glade dance upon the sea,
Its lunar light then called to me.
I swim upwards, toward the light,
Emerging neath a starlit night.
No longer chased or hunted,
Zeus had not got what he wanted.
The light of moon revealed to me,
My body was, at long last, free.
I did not know, Poseidon dwell,
In the water where I fell.
The ill-tempered, violent God of sea,
Then set his lustful gaze on me.
Though tired and frail from Zeus's chase,
I knew, again, I must efface.
I change my body, once again,
To float away from his domain.
I become an island, drifting free,
No pillars fix me to the sea.
But I did not anticipate,
A rootless islands withered state.
Lack of roots cause lack of growth,
Which would invoke perceivers loathe.
It saddens me that I shall be,
Floating, drifting, aimlessly.
Although my beauty shall be veiled,
Both Gods had lost whilst I prevailed.
Somehow, I hope that I endure,
Someday be anchored to its floor.

ILLUSION

Mythology speaks of my island,
Its wilting and withering state,
But the truth of the matter, dear reader,
Is the island and I correlate.

I was lost and adrift, like the island,
Without a fixed place of abode,
My heart, that once loved, was left broken,
Over time it began to corrode.

Our thread that was interconnected,
Was cut when Zeus took him away,
I believed it would hold all eternity,
Then I watched it unravel and fray.

There is no sound when your heart breaks,
But the pain shall endure, evermore,
The stars dimmed their light when it happened that night,
They were grieved by my tears that pour.

I had lost the one man I revered,
Then was forced, by the lustful, to flee,
When both had come near, I was quailed into fear,
Rearranged, because they had changed me.

So, the island is just an illusion,
A projection of my misery,
Rootless, alone, disparaged, I roam,
As the tears, from my pain, form the sea.

LETO

Leto was a goddess of womanly demure,
She kept her beauty veiled, concealed,
And vowed that it stay unrevealed,
To keep her fair and pure.
The reason for the veil she wore,
Was the power that her beauty yield,
For it shall lure men if revealed,
Who would implore for more.

But Zeus had seen her beauty, and had fallen for her grace,
He lusted for the sister of the one he once pursued,
For he was so enamoured by the beauty of her face,
But their love affair concluded once a pregnancy ensued,
And so began the vengeful, wrathful chase,
As Hera forced her into solitude.

ZEUS AND LETO

Your words of longing, love, and lust,
Embed within my heart,
Your promises envelop trust,
And I loved you from the start.

Every word that you impart,
Is said in softened tone,
I could not bear it if we part,
My love for you has grown.

I cannot bare to be alone,
Without you, I despair,
Your hand was made to fit my own,
Albeit through affair.

I love you; I adore you, and upon the stars, I wish,
That you be mine, is all I ask, for all I want is this.

HERA

You shall not break my heart again,
Too many times before,
Your infidelity caused pain.

Each time it left me in disdain,
But it shall hurt no more,
You shall not break my heart again.

Can you not see it wane?
With everything my heart endure,
Your infidelity caused pain.

You never change, always the same,
Deceit is at your core,
You shall not break my heart again.

You failed me, though I tried in vain,
And I am broken on the floor,
Your infidelity caused pain.

My mind resolved, I ascertain,
The man I loved, I now abhor,
You shall not break my heart again,
Your infidelity caused pain.

THE PROMISE

I am destitute and desperate,
For the wife of Zeus forebode,
Any place of land, or sea, or sky,
To offer me abode.
She swore that they should feel her wrath,
If any disobey,
And quelled by fear, they each adhere,
And none would let me stay.

I carry Zeus's children,
Both of which, shall soon be born,
So, I am seeking for the refuge,
From one who fears not, Hera's scorn.
I can see your isle is withered,
It is barren, disreputes,
But I promise if you let me stay,
It shall flourish from its roots.

The sea had brought me to you,
For, like you, I roam alone,
Both here because the thunder God,
Desired us for his own.
But my children shall be venerated,
If this place shall shield them both,
And I promise that if you accede,
They shall grant enduring growth.

I beg of you, Asteria, my sister and my friend,
To let me have my children here,
And your island shall transcend.

PILLARS

Leto made a promise,
In exchange for sanctuary,
That my island would astonish,
And be fixed within the sea.

Pillars root me to the sea,
Apollo made it so,
The son of Zeus had anchored me,
To sea, to thrive and grow.

Now here it stood, to be revered,
The island he called home,
No longer ridiculed or sneered,
Or drifting seas alone.

Its pillars bind me to the sea,
And confinement sets my island free.

APOLLO

Leto held her son, Apollo,
Moments after birth,
The God of sun, of light, of poetry,
Of so many things of worth.
His golden hair was long and strong,
And paralleled the sun.
Around his head were laurel leaves,
For this victorious little one.

'Apollo', spoke Leto,
'I know that you shall be,
A handsome God of virtue,
For this is your destiny.
One of the twelve Olympians,
Within the pantheon,
Befitting for the son of Zeus,
Who shines alike the sun.
Your gifts are constant, limitless,
Innumerable and sure,
You have aptitude for archery,
And your music shall allure.
You can bring disease or choose to heal,
And play the golden lyre,
You can grant the gift of prophecy,
To mortals who enquire'.

Apollo listened to these words,
Of power and prophecy,
He dreamt that day, beneath sunrays,
About his destiny.

ARTEMIS

Leto held her daughter, Artemis,
Moments after birth,
The goddess of the wild, the moon,
And huntress of the earth.
Her hair and eyes were silver-blonde,
And paralleled the moon.
Impressed upon her little brow,
She wore a silver lune.

'Artemis', spoke Leto.
'I know that you shall grow,
Formidable in battle,
With your quiver, arrows, bow.
One of the twelve Olympians,
Within the pantheon,
A rightful place for one of grace,
Enduring thereupon.
Your gifts are endless, boundless,
Infinite and vast,
You can form a constellation,
From any that have passed.
You can transform to an animal,
See through dark, when all are blind,
And control the lives of wildlife,
Through the power of your mind'.

Artemis had heard these words,
Of love and prophecy,
She dreamt that night, beneath moonlight,
About her destiny.

SIX WISHES

'My daughter', Zeus said lovingly,
To Artemis, upon his knee,
'Now that you are the age of three,
What does thy heart wish for?'.
'Father', she said longingly,
'Six wishes I desire from thee,
Each one means a great deal to me,
I shall not ask for more.

The first wish is that I may be,
Chaste for all eternity.
The second wish is I be known,
By other names, beyond my own.
The third wish is that you bestow,
A tunic, arrows, and a bow.
The fourth wish is that I bring light,
Phaesporia in darkened night.
The fifth wish is for company,
From sixty nymphs who dwell at sea.
The sixth wish is that I attain,
Each mountain to be my domain'.

'Artemis', Zeus said amused,
'Every wish that you have used,
Clearly comes from one bemused,
So, each I shall fulfil'.
'Father', she said, so enthused,
I am grateful that none were refused,
For, though I am young, I am not confused,
And each wish be my will'.

ANCESTORS

Ancestors dwell in the canvas of night,
Nocturnal, eternal, they shower with light,
Calming tired eyes with the lull of their glow,
Every star in the sky has descendants below.
Souls of our ancestors twinkle above,
They listen and glisten for people they love.
Only the darkness can bring them to light,
Revealing themselves on a black sky at night,
Single soul stars that align and shine bright.

PILLOW THOUGHTS

I.

The sky at night is so serene,
Laden with its stars,
And stardust from the brightest one,
Draws hearts around my scars.

II.

Souls are anchored to the stars,
Ancestral light pertain,
That every star within the sky,
Each bear a mortal name.

III.

Small stars quietly fade away,
They dwindle in the night,
Expending all their hydrogen,
They die, which dims their light.

IV.

Colossal stars cause supernovas,
Once its hydrogen has expend,
Their explosion brings new star formations,
So, their death is not the end.

V.

There are one hundred thousand million stars,
Just in the Milky Way,
If each one could be seen,
The night sky would gleam,
In a dazzling, golden display.

VI.

It takes millions of years for the light of the stars,
To appear and be seen when they shine,
So, to look at them is like you are looking,
One hundred thousand years back in time.

VII.

The brightest star in the night sky,
Is 8.6 lightyears away,
A binary star called Sirius,
The 'dog-star' of the Milky Way.

VIII.

There are 88-star constellations,
And 48 of these are Greek,
These are patterns that trace the distance and space,
Between stars that are ancient, antique.

IX.

The Rosette Nebula is a large star,
With a name, hue, and shape of a rose,
4 million years old, and a sight to behold,
For it shines pink and red when it glows.

X.

96% of the universe,
And its secrets have yet to be known,
But the 4% found, overawe, and astound,
So, just imagine what is yet to be shown.

STARS ARE OUR AFFINITY

Stars are our affinity. You told me long ago,
That you matched each to a reason,
As to why you love me so.
Remember when we saw that star,
Shooting in the sky?

And we made wishes on it as it,
Raced and passed us by.
Every time I look at stars, I think only of you,

Our love was formed beneath them,
Underneath their golden hue.
Romantically we were,

Aligned, our constellation shone,
Forever mine, forever yours,
Forever we are one.
I cannot tell the future,
Nor should I question fate,
I still wish on the brightest star I see,
To emanate. I wish for you, and they know,
You are more than worth the wait.

'Do you see a falling star?
Or hear the quails call?
Then Asteria is fleeing,
And evading Zeus's thrall'.

SELENE

THE STORY OF SELENE

Meet Selene, the goddess of the moon,
With her carriage, lunar white,
Who drives the moon between the stars,
And holds it there each night.

Selene epitomized the moon,
With skin so pale and fair,
As the canvas of the midnight sky,
Blend with her raven hair.

Her father was Hyperion,
The God of heavens light,
And her mother was the goddess Theia,
A Titaness of sight.

Selene had many love affairs,
With Gods that she allure,
But held back her heart conservedly,
For love that would endure.

Her soulmate came in mortal form,
A man who caught her sight,
A shepherd laid beneath her,
Who had set her heart alight.

Her tale is melancholic,
But her love for him ran deep,
On moonless nights she goes to him,
To the one she watches sleep.

ENDYMION

Beneath the stars his beauty glows,
The shepherd lost in deep repose,
Come dark, she drives the moon through night,
'Twas only he, who caught her sight.
He slumbered with tranquility, whilst longing immortality,
And this will surely come to be if she accede his plight.

Within the skies, she watched him sleep,
The mortal lost to dreams,
She willed the night to soon appear,
For he rest beneath her beams.
She watched him with affection,
Whilst she gaze in his direction,
And she longed for his protection,
As he slumbered so serene.

Selene then cast the moon aside,
To see her lover close,
His beauty had enchanted her, albeit in repose.
She longed for time to falter, so, his beauty could not alter,
Only this, could then console her,
If his beauty should be froze.

So, Selene had asked another,
To grant eternal sleep,
Upon this simple shepherd,
Who, before her slumbered deep.
The one she asked, relented,
With the shepherds' fate cemented,
And his ageing was prevented, whilst he forever lay asleep.

MOONLESS NIGHTS

Between the stars, I watch him,
As he slumbers neath my gaze,
A simple shepherd sleeping,
Whilst his flock serenely graze.

How curious he made me,
As he lay in deep repose,
I watch him from the distance,
But I long to see him close.

I descend and trail the moon behind,
Leaving only starlit skies,
Perchance if I tread quietly,
I shall not wake the one who lies.

My naked feet embed the earth,
And I set the moon aside,
Then trace in silence to the man,
I yearn to be beside.

Mournful for the moonless sky,
And the emptiness above,
Yet conflicted, for my heart impelled,
I seek the one I love.

Then, I see him laid before me,
And my guilt is quickly seized,
By the beaty of this shepherd,
As I long for time to freeze.

ENAMOURED

Endymion enamoured me,

None but he exist,

A man whose beauty calls to me,

My heart cannot resist.

Only he distracts me,

Underneath my moon,

Reposing and disclosing,

Exposing and invoking,

Dreaming and devoting,

By his side I feel attune.

Yearning for his love and touch,

Each night I watch him sleep,

No mortal ever caught my gaze,

Distracted me like he.

Yes, he had all consumed my mind,

My heart held him transfixed,

I longed to be the,

Only one, for there could be no other man,

No name but Endymion from my lips.

ZEUS

I held your naked body,
And appeased your aching heart,
Our love affair shall never fade,
I believed none could depart.

But I fear a mortal caught my gaze,
A man my eyes unearth,
He slumbers deep below my moon,
Upon a mound of earth.

He captivates me nightly,
And distracts my heart and mind,
No moon shall paint the midnight sky,
But for him, I am blind.

My love for him is ethereal,
As his beauty haunts my eyes,
But morality is ephemeral,
For the fates decree each dies.

I long to see him every night,
But time will not be kind,
I have a fear, the passing years,
Will ravage as designed.

So, I ask my former lover,
Zeus, please hear my plea,
And grant him deep, eternal sleep,
And immortality.

MOON GODDESS

She wore a gown of silver,
A hue that matched the moon,
Her raven hair, like midnight air,
Was embellished with a lune.

Her skin was pale and luminous,
Like moon glade cast to sea,
Her gentle eyes told lullabies,
That beguile the ones who see.

Each night she drove a chariot,
Across the darkened night,
To bring the moon and night attune,
Pulled by two steeds of white.

She brings the moon to dead of night,
Her role, through time, runs deep,
The sun descends and she ascends,
To grant the gift of sleep.

Selene is the epitome,
Of lunar phase and time,
Her beauty grows when nighttime shows,
Primordial, divine.

But her heart was ever searching,
For the one in deep repose,
For he shall be, eternally,
The reason why she glows.

HE ECLIPSED HER

He eclipsed her, the shepherd,
That Selene watched through the night,
As he slumbered deep below her,
In his cave of moonstone white.

Though he slumbered for eternity,
in silence, with no voice,
He still begged of her to visit,
Love compelled; she had no choice.

So, her chariot descended,
With the moon then cast aside,
And the darkened sky was painted,
With only stars to map its guide.

He unknowingly eclipsed her,
As he lay in slumber, deep,
Her light, concealed and hidden,
For the one she watches sleep.

He was all Selene could think about,
Endymion and his light,
And when he would eclipse her mind,
She brought forth a moonless night.

She could only think of holding him,
All others dissipate,
He eclipsed her which concealed the moon,
And only his light emanate.

SHADOWS

Our love was cloaked in shadows,
In the darkness of the night,
A secret hidden from the world,
That I longed to bring to light.

The moon was our affinity,
As we lay beneath its glow,
The world asleep, and silence,
With time elapsing slow.

I loved you in the darkness,
Where no one's eyes could see,
As you filled my head with splendid words,
Of a future that could be.

In those moments that you held me,
How I longed for time to pause,
For while the world was put to sleep,
My heart was freely yours.

But love concealed by shadows,
Could it ever see the light?
Would fate align your heart to mine?
Could we make it past the night?

I love you, irregardless,
And shall wait for all of time,
In the hope the shadows dissipate,
So, I can, one day, say you are mine.

ANATOLIA

There is a cave in Anatolia,
With walls of painted white,
Adorned with precious moonstones,
That illuminate at night.

This cave withholds a secret,
For inside its walls there lay,
A mortal turned immortal man,
Who sleeps each passing day.

The cave is watched by nymphai,
When sunlight reigns the skies,
But come the night, Selene descends,
And her love for him reprise.

This cave is very sacred,
As the one who dwells within,
Was lover to the moon goddess,
Who descent only for him.

This cave provided sanctuary,
To the man that she adore,
A truly sacred, special place,
Where her love for him endure.

This cave of white lay hidden,
On a mountain, all alone,
And its precious walls of beauty,
Paralleled her lovers own.

INTOXICATED

You intoxicate me!

Every word from your lips,
As each syllable drips,
Secrecy.
Your honeyed words spill,
And each one fills me with,
Reverie.

You intoxicate me!

As your tongue would caress,
Gently teasing my breasts,
Sensuality.
You set me alight,
And my body ignite,
Volcanically.

You intoxicate me!

When you enter me slow,
And I feel as your grow,
Exponentially.
With our bodies entwined,
As we both lay aligned,
Synchronically.

You intoxicate me!

HELIOS

'Helios', she begged him,
'My brother of the sun,
Please drive the moon for me tonight,
As I go to Endymion.
My heart hurts from his absence,
And this pain shall not efface,
Although he doze in sweet repose,
I yearn to see his face.
I think only of my lover,
For he consumes my mind,
But the moon must paint the midnight sky,
For without it, earth be blind.
I long to lay beside him,
Where we two are not apart,
Please drive the moon for me tonight, I beg with longing heart'.

'Selene', her brother answered,
'My sister of the moon,
I shall oblige you once again,
And take your reigns from noon.
But my sun is so lethargic,
And the Gods have seen the change,
They are questioning my tiredness,
Asking why the sun acts strange.
They will not see rhyme nor reason
If they find that you descend,
You must make a choice, your lover?
Or the moon? For one must end.
Spend tonight with your immortal,
Whilst I shall do your task,
But the difficulty of it begs, that you no longer ask'.

SEDUCED

'Come to me' she whispered,
As her fingers trace his chest,
'I shall satiate your tongue,
Whilst your hands explore my breasts.
Surrender to desire,
And take me for your own,
I long to feel you deep within,
And yearn to hear you moan.
My body aches to feel your touch,
And craves your naked form,
Unwaveringly resolute,
To pleasure you till morn.
Come to me with ardour,
And slip beneath my sheet,
Embrace the warmth of pleasure,
As our bodies bask in heat.
Grasp my hips with passion,
And gaze deep within my eyes,
Caress my tongue, and bite my lip,
For mine shall then reprise.
Cover me completely,
As our bodies intertwine,
Allow yourself the sweet release,
That comes from being mine.
I ache for you to enter me,
For our bodies to unite,
So, come to me, my darling,
If only for tonight'.

PAN

'Your beauty has ensnared me', Pan said with lustful voice,
'Selene, you captivate me, I am compelled without a choice.
I can offer you two oxen, each one pearlescent white,
If you shall take my wanton hand and lay with me tonight.
I ask that you accept me, for our bodies to entwine,
Please take the gifts I give you, in exchange for being mine'.

'Pan', she cooed seductively, 'I accept what you propose,
I shall take your gift of oxen and be with you in repose.
You offer me a wanton hand, and beg for our embrace,
Our bodies shall both intertwine, and others shall efface.
I accept you and your yearning, for I am lonely too,
I shall be with you this coming night and see the evening through'.

'My dear Selene', he answered, 'to your beauty, none compare,
You call to me like sand to sea, like stars to midnight air.
I long to kiss your gracious neck, as our bodies both align,
Though I know this is ephemeral and short lived shall be our time.
But I offer you a night of pleasure, a thing we both desire,
You hold the match, my dear Selene, come light my dormant fire.

'Oh Pan' she cried elated, 'I can sense your loneliness,
I see the passion in your eyes, as your hands long to caress.
I know that lonesome feeling, and my heart is yearning too,
Your words are like a magnet, each compelling me to you.
Do not fear my rejection, for those words shall not be said,
The match I hold shall soon alight the flame within your bed'.

BETWEEN THE STARS

Between the stars, she emanates,
Each night she shall appear,
To transform the sky of darkness,
With the magic of her sphere.
Ever changing and eternal,
Ever loving and maternal,
Never failing and nocturnal,

Time evades when she is here.
Her milky light attunes the night,
Each star shines with her grace,

She grants the gift of sleep to those,
That gaze upon her face,
And with her gentle lullaby,
Reposing mortals softly lie,
Selene holds them in embrace.

SELENITE

Its name derives from her,
A suffix for Selene,
A gypsum crystal, milky white,
Translucent and serene.

Selenite portrays the moon,
With its luminescent tone,
And the goddesses own energy,
Sits embedded in this stone.

This crystal, like the moon above,
Emits a pure white light,
A comforting and tranquil glow,
Dispelling darkness from the night.

Selenite holds affinity,
With the goddess of the moon,
Like her, it clears, it calms, it comforts,
And it heals through its illume.

It epitomizes love and truth,
This crystal for the mind,
Its beauty parallels her own,
And its virtue just as kind.

This crystal is enveloped,
And protected by Selene,
A sacred stone, that those who own,
Find it keeps the mind serene.

THE ALCHEMIST

There he sleeps, eternal,

He is an alchemist, they say,

Ever youthful, ever beautiful,

And immortal he shall stay.

Listen closely to the silence,

Close your mind and you shall hear,

How the magic of his slumber,

Enchants your heart to draw you near.

Moonlight cloaks him whilst reposing,

It is how he stays attune,

Sleeping, dreaming, drinking, soaking,

The elixir of the moon.

PHASES

She is the moon, and he is earth,
She orbits round his sphere,
Tidally locked to only him,
As he makes her light appear.

She goes through many phases,
There are eight that she maintains,
And perceptions always alter,
Based on where her lover reigns.

It takes twenty-nine point five days,
To transition through each phase,
But each one impart a message,
Based on what her light conveys:

The first phase is the new moon,
New beginnings will unfold,
The second, waxing crescent moon,
Allow intentions to be mould,
The third is the first quarter moon,
A time you can achieve,
The fourth, the waxing gibbous moon,
Observe this and believe.
The fifth phase is the full moon,
A chance to be content.
The sixth, the waning gibbous moon,
Be grateful and assent.
The seventh, the third quarter moon,
Release what needs to go.
The eighth, the waning crescent moon,
Surrender through her glow.

THE NEW MOON

The darkness envelops her,
She is hidden, unfound,
Consumed by her absence of light,
She is bound.

The silence besets her,
She is unable to quell,
The feeling of sadness,
That she longs to expel.

The sun does not warm her,
Though both are aligned,
The stars are no comfort,
To their light, she is blind.

The earth sees her absence,
But still, they repose,
As she hides in the darkness,
Secreting her woes.

The sadness consumes her,
And though, far from full,
She waits ever patient,
Till the night she can lull.

The night sky is painted,
Without her divine,
But this phase is temporal,
One night soon, she shall shine.

REFLECTION

Our love would show through starlight,
Reflected in ancestral light,
Concealed by day, revealed at night,
Shown only to the moon.

Our lips would lock at midnight,
Stolen kisses during twilight,
Shadow cuddles under lunar light,
Viewed only by the moon.

Our hands would roam at stoplights,
Lustful touch derived from foresight,
Tongues caress as mouths are airtight,
Beneath the crescent moon.

Our hearts would burn like firelight,
Fiery, frenzied embers dancing bright,
Kindle flames we both ignite,
Below the tranquil moon.

Our eyes would lock then incite,
Lustful glances sent to invite,
Secret longing for the rewrite,
Of our future past the moon.

SELENOPHILE

She is a selenophile. A goddess of night,
Beautiful and powerful,
As she bathes in lunar light.

She is an astrophile. A lover of the stars,
Nocturnal and eternal,
As she glows infinite, and sparse.

She is a nyctophile. A dreamer of the night,
Celestial and primordial,
As she watch the sky ignite.

She is an umbraphile. A seeker of eclipse,
Ancestral and archaic,
As she looks in awe, transfixed.

She is an autophile. A girl of solitude,
Serenity and tranquility,
As she yearns to be seclude.

She is a pluviophile. A lover of the rain,
Transcendental and torrential,
As she hides her tears of pain.

She is everything and nothing,
But her love shall never wane,
For the moon, the stars, the night, the eclipse,
The silence, and the rain.

'Do you see a moonless sky?
No luminescent beams?
Then Selene is with her lover,
Her immortal lost to dreams.'

NYX

THE STORY OF NYX

Meet Nyx, the goddess of the night,
Revered, and feared, and awed,
Who dwells within the underworld,
Where all evil souls are stored.

Nyx was born to Chaos,
An aptly titled name,
He was born at the dawn of creation,
And his daughter was the same.

Her consort was Erebus,
A God of darkness, and of mist,
And they bore many children,
Through their concupiscent tryst.

She invoke a fear, so frightening,
Which is evident in her tale,
The oldest goddess in Greek myth,
Only she could make Zeus quail.

The cloak she wears, conceals the sky,
As she takes to flight each night,
And in her chariot of black,
She eradicates the light.

But her story is integral,
One to last forevermore,
A tale of darkness, and of power,
Which ensure that Nyx, endure.

EREBUS

Erebus,

We were born at the dawn of creation,
Two lovers, whose thread was,
Combined,
Destined and fated, no others,
Could entangle, but stay so,
Aligned.

Erebus, my consort of darkness,
My brother, and lover,
Assigned,
We were born before time was created,
As the offspring that Chaos,
Designed.

We reside in the dwelling of Hades,
And together, we live,
Unconfined,
Two lovers who reign over darkness,
Sister, brother, and lovers,
Defined.

Erebus, I seek only your hand,
And to all other Gods, I am,
Blind,
For you are my immortal lover,
And to only you, I am,
Inclined.

BENEATH THE SHEETS

Beneath the sheets, embracing,

Every fingertip was tracing,

Naked bodies, interlacing,

Every touch was so displacing,

As their tongues were fast and chasing,

Thoughts of others were effacing,

Heartbeats pounding, hard and racing,

They were lost beneath the sheets.

His kiss was so sedating,

Each one sexual, collating,

She breathed heavily, awaiting,

He withdrew, and left her waiting,

Every touch left her pulsating,

Every kiss, intoxicating,

Tracing fingers, circulating,

So each night, their lust repeats.

HER CHILDREN

Nyx and Erebus,
Had many children together,
Some were evil, some were pure,
Some were feared, some revered,
Some were hated, some adored,
Some awe-inspired, some terrified,
Some brought chaos, some played tricks,
Let me introduce them to you,
Meet the seventeen children of Nyx.

Aether:

Aether was known as the goddess of air,
A primordial deity, refined,
Adored by most mortals, goddesses, and Gods,
For she was pure, she was fair, and was kind.

Hemera:

Hemera was the goddess of day,
A primordial deity of light,
She moved in counterpart to Nyx,
For she gave the earth, sunlight.

The Oneiroi:

The Oneiroi were her one thousand sons,
Winged spirits of darkness and dreams,
They would give prophesies, to mortals who sleep,
But these were not always what they seem.

The Keres:

The Keres were her one thousand daughters,
Death spirits of violence and gore,
They were drawn towards blood, as it spills on the mud,
Of the ground used for battles and war.

The Moirai:

The Fates, also known as the Moirai,
Were three sisters who each govern fate,
These were Clotho, and Lachesis, and Atropos,
And they control each mortals own state.

Hypnos:

Hypnos, was the God of sleep,
And this deity could hypnotize,
He was said to be calm and quite gentle,
As he helped those in need, close their eyes.

Geras:

Geras was the God of elderly age,
And he resides at the underworld gates,
Alongside disease, anxiety, and grief,
He stands there with these and he waits.

Oizys:

Oizys was the goddess of misery,
Of heartbreak, of pain, and of woe,
Whenever this goddess appears, all be warned,
Any tears left unspilled, overflow.

Momus:

Momus was God of satire, and blame,
And also the twin of Oizys,
He inflicted such dread, if he got in your head,
As he kept mortals held back from peace.

Eris:

Eris was the goddess of chaos,
Discord, disorder, and strife,
And she brought down a wrath so tumultuous,
Which reigned terror on all mortal life.

Nemesis:

Nemesis, goddess of retribution,
Enacted revenge against those,
Who succumb to their pride, or act in deride,
Or their arrogant vanity shows.

Philotes:

Philotes, the goddess of affection,
Of friendship and sexuality,
Was not like her siblings or parents,
For her spirit was warm and carefree.

Apate:

Apate, the goddess of deception,
Was a trickster, who was guile, and a cheat,
She escaped from the box of Pandora,
And was the embodiment of lies and deceit.

The Hesperides:

The Hesperides were her three daughters,
These were Aegle, Erytheis, and Hespere,
They were Nymphs of the gold light of sunset,
And each spoke in a dulcet tone, clear.

Moros:

Moros was the God of destruction,
And doom, as he impend and wait,
He was vengeful, and spiteful, and hateful,
Driving mortals to their deadly fate.

Thanatos:

Thanatos, was the God of death,
And would appear before the dead,
To take their souls to the underworld,
Once the Fates had cut their thread.

Charon:

Charon became Hades ferryman,
And it was he who ferried the deceased,
Down the river that led to the underworld,
But only if they had a coin for his fees.

BLANKET OF STARS

Before your bed,

Lay a blanket of stars,

And they glitter, and glisten,

Numberless, not sparse.

Kaleidoscopically flitting,

Each dazzle like gold,

They are gifts from Asteria, for

Our eyes to behold.

Flickering softly, they are,

Scatteredly cast, and,

This blanket of stars,

All night long shall last.

Remember that each,

Star, is a soul who has passed.

HAND IN HAND WITH EREBUS

'Erebus',
She beckoned him,
Reaching out for his hand,
'Let us venture from Tartarus,
And bring darkness to land'.

She had planned,
To conceal,
The light sky with her cloak,
To cast darkness for mortals,
Till each had awoke.

As she spoke,
He acceded,
And their fingers aligned,
They ascent from the underworld,
To make all of earth blind.

Both combined,
Brought forth chaos,
As they both paint the night,
Only Selene, and Asteria,
Could break through with their light.

They shone bright,
Through the darkness,
Nyx and Erebus provoke,
Till they descent to the underworld,
And with them, goes her cloak.

SOLIVAGENT

She was a solivagant,
As she wandered at night,
She loved stardust, and nightfall,
Darkness, and moonlight.

She sought solace,
When dark reigned up high,
She loved starlight that glitters,
Like art in the sky.

She was peaceful,
When Nyx cast her cloak,
She loved silence and lull,
That only she could invoke.

She felt comfort,
Like time had just froze,
She loved wandering neath,
Selene's moon that arose.

She found healing,
Through the lull of the stars,
She loved the touch of Asteria,
Which trace gold round her scars.

She was a solivagant,
And though on her own,
She loved to wander at night,
For she was never alone.

STAR FILLED CLOAK

She wears her star filled cloak each night,

That is thrown over earth, over sky,

And it glimmers and glistens, with glittering light,

Revealing their glow way up high.

For while mortals are lulled, and reposing,

In the sky, Nyx shall unfurl her cloak,

Light concealed, with not one ray exposing,

Littered stars flit, till earth has awoke.

Every night, Nyx appears from the shadows,

Darkness come as this goddess arrives,

Cascading her cloak, and it billows,

Laid out with its stars in the skies,

Obscuring the light,

A star filled cloak of the night,

Keeping it there until the sunrise.

EMBODIMENT OF NIGHT

Goddess Nyx embodies,
The night,
With her four-horse draw carriage,
She would take
To flight,
A goddess with cloak,
That could drown out,
The light.

At twilight, every night,
She ascend,
With horses, carriage, and cloak,
To a sky that impend,
A cloak full of stars,
With a brightness they lend.
At the end of the night,
They retreat,

She pulls back her four horses,
Which in turn pulls back,
The sheet,
That covers the sky,
And all darkness deplete.
Every night she repeats,
The same thing,

Across earth at twilight,
Nyx would appear and bring,
A dark sky ahead,
For mortals reposing.

TARTARUS

The fire was hot, and scolding,
Flames enfolding, embers bolting,
And the heat was, so revolting,
This alone caused fear, and dread,
For this place was dark, depressing,
Soul oppressing, mind distressing,
And this place I am addressing,
Is the dwelling of the dead.

It was torturous, and tainted,
Bloodstained painted, and acquainted,
By the souls it emanated,
From the fire that burns, and blinds,
For this place held, the immoral,
The unmoral, the amoral,
Every soul would fight and quarrel,
Eternally they are confined.

An abyss of death, constriction,
Of affliction, dereliction,
She could see beyond depiction,
See beyond what she was shown,
And though it was cruel, corrupted,
It disrupted and flames erupted,
Nyx lived here uninterrupted,
And she calls Tartarus, home.

CRONUS

Cronus was the God of time,
And was revered and cheered by all,
But his greed would lead to dreadful deeds,
That result in his downfall.

His father was Uranus,
The Titan God of sky,
His mother Gaia was the goddess,
Of earth and all that underlie.

Cronus overthrew his father,
So that he may rule and reign,
Then he wed his sister, Rhea,
But soon after caused her pain.

The moment he gained power,
Peace on all of earth unfold,
Mortals lived a carefree, healthy life,
And they lived till they were old.

But the God was too inquisitive,
He yearned to know his fate,
Which led to deadly consequences,
For his children, whom he ate.

The story you are about to hear,
Is full of woe and pain,
It will tell of the God Cronus,
And how he ended up in chains.

ORACLES

Smoke encircled,
Dark clouds formed,
Around the cave of the goddess,
Who brought forth the storm,
She could warn,
And foretell,
Those who sought future knowledge,
Would seek out her spell,
Many fell,
On the way,
So concerned by an uncertain future,
Before them that lay.
On this day,
Cronus came,
To the Adyton of Nyx, as he entered the cave,
Through the rain,
She explain,
That one day,
A child of his own, would have him overthrown,
They would slay.
He display,
His own strife,
And he vowed to prevent this,
Even if it meant taking their life.
Soon his wife,
Would be pained,
For he would swallow his children at birth,
To ensure he still reigned.

And as a result of the oracle given by Nyx,
Cronus changed.

BABY BLANKET

Rhea held her children close,
As tears laced her eyes,
She gaze upon the five of them,
Aware of their demise.

Her husband, Cronus, heard a prophecy,
That he would be overthrown,
And he told his wife it would be by,
One of the five they own.

She had listened to his intentions,
And as he spoke, he made it clear,
That she should not fight against him,
And he forced her to adhere.

Rhea watched him gather Hestia,
And swallow her before her eyes,
Then he took Demeter,
Who let out such fearful cries.

Cronus swallowed Hera,
Which then only left their boys,
Then he swallowed Hades,
As Rhea watched without a choice.

Their remaining son, Poseidon,
Was bundled by her chest,
But Cronus took him forcefully,
And his fate was like the rest.

Rhea was numb and broken,
Now a mother with no child,
She had watched the man, she once adored,
Change into something wild.

She did not tell her husband,
Of their sixth child, to be born,
For she knew his fate would be the same,
Just another child to mourn.

Once Cronus heard of baby Zeus,
He ordered for the boy,
But Rhea wrapped a boulder,
In a blanket, as a ploy.

Cronus swallowed without looking,
Then Rhea hid the child in Crete,
Asking nine Nymphs to watch over him,
Who accede to her deceit.

On Mount Dicte, he was protected,
In the safety of their care,
But any chance that Rhea had,
She would go to visit there.

But she knew one day that Zeus would grow,
And seek the one who ate,
His brothers and his sisters,
So till that day, she would wait.

ADRASTEIA

In the arms of Adrasteia, Zeus was safe,
For she nourished him with honey, in this cave.
A mountain Nymph, who loved the son of Rhea,
And ensured he suckled milk from Amalthea.
Adrasteia was goddess of certain fate,
Aphrodite was her mother, they correlate,
For she loved the boy entrusted to her care,
And demonstrated this whilst he was there.
Years rolled by as Zeus transformed into a man,
And he spoke to Adrasteia of his plan,
He would wage a war with Cronus, undiscerned,
Which would lead to all his siblings being returned.
Adrasteia was aggrieved to say goodbye,
But Zeus made her a constellation in the sky,
He was grateful for the care that she had shown,
Then he left the cave in Crete to claim his throne.
Zeus tricked Cronus in a guise, that he design,
And became his own cupbearer, serving wine.
He laced the glass with herbs of potency,
Telling his father of the power he would see.
He watched as Cronus took the glass and sip,
In seconds, he was keeling, and was sick.
The boulder came out first, then one by one,
The five children that he ate, were free to run,
And so began the Titanomachy,
As Zeus defeat his father, publicly.
Cronus was thrown into the cave of Nyx,
Forever bound in chains, and wall affixed.

URSA MAJOR

Adrasteia's constellation,
Formed in the northern sky,
And she watched each star appearing,
As they glittered way up high.

Her constellation – Ursa Major,
Is Latin for 'great bear',
To Greeks, a bear is symbolism,
For both motherhood, and care.

She watched the Ursa Major,
In the sky as it augment,
And Adrasteia's constellation,
Took up 3.102%.

It was beautiful, and glistened,
Reflecting stardust in her eyes,
Adrasteia's constellation,
Was the third largest in the sky.

Fashioned with 135 stars,
Each one had a glistening hue,
7 of which, were an asterism,
That connect her to other stars too.

She had raised Zeus from an infant,
Had nourished him with love,
So he ensured, that she endured,
Immortal, up above.

DRUNK ON HONEY

Cronus was intoxicated,
He was lost in deep repose,
Chained to the wall of Nyx's cave,
Bound tight, nakedly posed.

Tricked by his son, he became enslaved,
In chains that could not break,
And was forced to drink a honey mix,
To make him never wake.

In his chains, he slumbered deeply,
Drunk on honey, Cronus dreams,
He was forced to witness horrors,
Of events yet to be seen.

These were torturous, and tainted,
Visions he could not withstand,
But the honey was too potent,
And it kept him in dreamland.

He described them in his stupor,
As she listened so transfixed,
Every prophecy Cronus described,
Was echoed, then, by Nyx.

She would chant these words of downfall,
To earth and all mankind,
And as she gave these auguries,
The universe danced, aligned.

HYPNOS

Her husband, Zeus, betrayed her,
She was desperate to avenge,
For Zeus's indiscretion,
And she ached to seek revenge.
She had learnt of Zeus, and Leto,
And the twins they both had bore,
And it tore her heart to pieces,
Like the countless times before.
She scoured earth for Hypnos,
Nyx's son, the God of sleep,
As her only chance for vengeance,
Would be if Zeus was slumbered deep.
Hypnos had the power to quell him,
To suppress him and subdue,
So that Hera could torment him,
For all that he had put her through.
She found Hypnos in the underworld,
And spoke of her intent,
But his dissuasion to the goddess failed,
For she would not relent.
So he placed him into deep repose,
But Zeus soon disengaged,
And he woke up conscious and aware,
Furious and enraged.
He would scour the earth for Hypnos,
And planned to kill him where he stood,
How dare he trick the God of sky,
Zeus was seeking for his blood.

REFUGE

He fled the God in fear,
Zeus was near, it was clear,
That Hypnos had interfered,
And adhered to Hera's ploy,
Now the God of sky was chasing,
Both were racing, Zeus was tracing,
Pacing all of earth to find him,
Find the one he would destroy.

He dropped from the sky descending,
Never ending, fear portending,
Intending to evade him,
And hide in the cave of Nyx,
For he knew Zeus feared his mother,
He uncover, and discover,
There was no other Zeus would turn from,
Only her gaze could transfix.

Hypnos reached the cave she dwell in,
She foretell in, souls indwelling,
And expelling any chance to die,
He hid in her domain.
When Zeus reached the cave, benighted,
Rage subsided, he was blighted,
And decided it would not be worth,
Her wrath, if he, remain.

LATE NIGHT COFFEE

Late night coffee, midnight thoughts,

And restless, weary mind,

This cup shall warm my frozen palms,

Each sip shall help unwind.

No other vice can quell my mind, as

I watch the sun deplete,

Giving way to Selene's moon, as

Helios makes his retreat.

Then I sip from this elixir,

Consume its warmth through woe,

Only the stars, conceal my scars,

For I drink beneath their glow,

Finding it bittersweet and soothing,

Every sip is so seducing,

Even though it is wrong, I know.

DEAD STARS

We are all dead stars:
The calcium in our bones,
The iron in our veins,
The oxygen we breathe,
The nitrogen in our brains,
The hydrogen in our bodies,
And the carbon we contain,
Were each formed in a star,
That the night sky maintain.
When the star had exploded,
We were all that remain,
As we dropped from the sky,
And we glittered like flames.
We are each made of stardust,
But the stars ascertain,
That though we share atoms,
We are unique through names.

'Do you see darkness approaching?'
Or sense dread in the night?
Then Nyx is in her carriage,
With her cloak, concealing light.'

CIRCE

THE STORY OF CIRCE

Meet Circe, pronounced 'ser-see',
A goddess and a witch,
An enchantress and a sorceress,
With the power to bewitch.

Circe's father was named Helios,
Who was the god of sun,
And her mother, Perse, an ocean nymph,
Where her magic roots came from.

She fell in love so many times,
But this love was not returned,
Rejection from the ones she loved,
Had left her feeling spurned.

There came a day, when jealous rage,
Had caused her own exile,
She was banished for eternity,
To Aeaea, a lonesome isle.

Now Circe was a gifted witch,
Who used a wand and wine,
With herbs and spells and potions,
That would transform men to swine.

Circe used her potent spell,
Each time that she was scorned,
Once you have Circe's affection,
Do not reject her, all be warned.

GLAUCUS

The sea god came to Circe,
With desperation in his heart,
He spoke of unrequited love,
And she listen as he impart.

He explained his love for Scylla,
A Naiad, cloaked with grace,
How he watched her from the water,
Captivated by her face.

Glaucus then told Circe,
How one day he swam too near,
Scylla happened on him watching,
And his looks filled her with fear.

Circe listened to his sorrow,
And acceded to his plight,
She would generate a potion,
That would make his love requite.

He was grateful and elated,
That his love would be returned,
And he told her just how fiercely,
His love for Scylla burned.

Circe watched him, so enchanted,
Inadvertently, she wished,
He could love her, just like Scylla,
Still, she promised to assist.

THE GIRL HE LOVES

The girl he loves is like a rose,

Her beauty blooms, each day it grows,

Each word for her, that he impart,

Gave thorns that pierced my bleeding heart.

Insatiable and undeterred,

Revealing how his feelings stirred,

Lost all sight of those who gaze,

He douse the fire that others blaze.

Each time her saw her, love grew more,

Lost to only her allure.

Only she, did he desire,

Veraciously, with love struck fire.

Every other, but her, he rebuffs,

So beautiful, the girl he loves.

JEALOUSY

'Stay here with me, forget her face,
All memories of her, shall erase,
My head, my heart, your love has turned,
Do not chase the one who spurned'.

Circe spoke the words above,
Declaring just how much she love,
The god of sea, who willingly,
Asked her to aid him with his plea.

'Trees shall root to ocean bed,
Before my love for Scylla shed,
And seaweed thrive on mountain top,
Before my love for her shall stop'.

Glaucus spoke unwelcome words,
And these enraged her once she heard,
So inflamed by his deride,
She devised a plan to lull her pride.

'Her beauty, I shall dissipate,
From nymph, to monster, fueled by hate,
All shall abhor this wretched whore,
Who haunts and taunts the ocean floor'.

She planned to taint where Scylla bathed,
To change the beauty Glaucus craved,
Into a creature that repel,
A monster formed from jealous spell.

POISON

He had left her,
Left her broken,
And a broken heart compel,
That she seek her retribution,
Through the power of a spell.

She would poison,
Poison Scylla,
In the pool the Naiad bathed,
And transform her from a beauty,
To a monster, sea enslaved.

He had poisoned,
Poisoned Circe,
Through rejection and disdain,
He had doused her flame of passion,
Which ignite her lust for pain.

She then poisoned,
Poisoned Scylla,
So consumed by jealousy,
She bore anger and resentment,
Towards this beauty in the sea.

She had left him,
Left him broken,
And a broken man decline,
He had lost the one he yearned for,
Now forever he shall pine.

EXILE

Her broken heart lay shattered,
It was tattered, all that mattered,
Was her plan for retribution,
For the one that she abhor,
But the consequence of jealousy,
And her potent extremity,
Had meant the witch be exiled,
To return home,
Nevermore.

Her rage then slowly faded,
It eliminated, dissipated,
Gone was any trace,
Of the anger she once bore,
But the consequence of jealousy,
Dishonesty, and treachery,
Would mean the witch would have to be,
In exile,
Evermore.

Her guilt then soon invaded,
It asphyxiated, desiccated,
Caused eternal banishment
From the homeland she adore.
This, the consequence of jealousy,
Admittedly, decidedly,
Regretfully unchangeable,
Hence exilement,
Forevermore.

THE WITCH'S HOUSE

On the island of Aeaea,
Lived a goddess in exile,
This sorceress, enchantress,
Built her home here on the isle.

The witch's house was lavish,
But behind its grand veneer,
Lay the truth of Circe's magic,
Over men who drew too near.

She would lure them to her dwelling,
And would tempt each man with wine,
Then once inebriated,
Waved her wand to make them swine.

The men lost all humanity,
And as pigs they would reside,
Domesticated, desiccated,
By the witch's side.

The goddess waited patiently,
For inquisitive men to call,
Amidst the forest, stood her house,
Where those who enter, fall.

GOSSAMER GOWN

She wore a gown of gossamer,
The colour of a rose,
Arousing all who come to call,
Seduced by what it shows.

It figure hugged her body,
Barely veiled her gentle skin,
And allure all men who saw her,
In this gown so sheer and thin.

It entice with such beguilement,
Would entrance and could possess,
All those who saw the gown she wore,
Longed for her to undress.

It embodied lust and passion,
As it curved around her hips,
And the men it hoaxed would all be coaxed,
To kiss her wanton lips.

It enamored and enchanted,
Captivated all who saw,
And those who strayed, betrayed, then stayed,
With her forevermore.

TEMPTRESS

Come to me, my darling,
Forget yourself awhile,
My lips shall drip with honeyed words,
While we both lay in exile.
Conceal the guilt you feel, my love,
But know this to be true,
The sweetness to pour from my lips,
Shall overspill for you.

Come taste my words of nectar,
For each one shall stir and rouse,
My lips shall drip with lustful scripts,
Sweet words that shall arouse.
Defer all thoughts of her, my love,
For ambrosia shall lure.
Alike the bee to pollen,
You shall fall for my allure.

Come stay with me in exile,
Where our bodies shall entwine,
My lips shall drip, their viscous grip,
Shall adhere your lips to mine.
Leave behind all memory,
Of the one you shall betray,
And come to me, in exile,
How I long for you to stay.

WITCHCRAFT

Mythology speaks of my stories,
Tells you tales of magic and spell,
But it rarely reveals the true story,
So, dear reader, allow me to dispel.

They speak of my talent with witchcraft,
How I transform the men I abhor,
Of my gift, as a witch and enchantress,
With the power to destroy through allure.

But I was a girl who was broken,
Each time I found love, I felt pain,
Every man offered lies and rejection,
And each blow left my heart in disdain.

I sought for a love so archaic,
Like the stars that embellish the sky,
But it dwindled with each passing sailor,
And it faded with every goodbye.

I did what I could to appease them,
But I could not get any to stay,
I fed them, bed them and begged them,
Then was forced to watch each sail away.

My heart had faced so much rejection,
That my eyes would run dry through the pain,
I offered myself to these sailors,
But their answer was always the same.

You see, they desired my body,
But my mind and my heart, they refused,
Seeking only a lustful companion,
With a body willing to be used.

My heart waned each time I would lose them,
As they boarded their vessel to leave,
And it broke me to stand there in exile,
As the sea, once again, watch me grieve.

I willed for a lover's acceptance,
And long that he stay by my side,
But not one could commit to affection,
Yet they each condescend and deride.

Love could not exist in exilement,
A lesson I learnt from the past,
And I determined that each passing sailor,
Would just lie and deceive like the last.

So, my heart turned to rock, like the island,
As my tears, from the past, filled the sea,
And my magic was taint and corrupted,
By the men who had hurt me, then flee.

I resolved, with my broken heart beating,
That my witchcraft shall be used to quell,
So, I used my enchantments to trick them,
And I safeguard my heart through a spell.

CHANNELING HER MAGIC

Her bones were cloaked in magic,
She was born a gifted witch,
With the power to transform herself,
Or any man she wished.

Her banishment to the island,
Meant she lived alone, confined,
In isolation, desolation,
Which poisoned Circe's mind.

Her body channeled magic,
But she used her gift to harm,
With potency and trickery,
She used it to disarm.

Her magic held dexterity,
Though she practiced through disdain,
For her mind sought retribution,
For the men who caused her pain.

Her heart was broken constantly,
And with each blow she received,
Her tears would flow from sorrow,
Over men she had believed.

So, the witch, her spells, her potions,
And the magic she impart,
Were channeled and perfected,
To conserve her broken heart.

CIRCE'S SPELL

'Welcome to Aeaea',
The goddess Circe said,
'How ravenous you all must be,
How in need of food and bed!
Come forth into my quarters,
Lay down your sailor cap,
How handsomely you all shall eat,
Before you take a nap,'

The sailors entered grateful,
For the reception they received.
The kindness of this sorceress,
Could barely be believed.
They ate with hastened vigour,
As she topped them up with wine,
Circe reveled in their gluttony,
Before she turned each man to swine.

Circe pulled her magic wand,
And spoke her potent spell:
'All you men who sit before me,
On Aeaea, from now, shall dwell.'
The wine she gave was laced with herbs,
Each glass she watched them swig,
Had turned each man from mortal form,
Into a subdued pig.

Circe watched the transformed men,
Who wailed and cried with woe,
She reveled in their misery,
'To the pigsty you shall go!'

DEADLY NIGHTSHADE

The bell-shaped flowers with purple hue,
Grew deep within her wood,
'Atropa Belladonna',
With its meaning understood:

'Atropa' comes from Atropos,
The eldest of the fates,
Who cut the string to mortal life,
Where death impends and waits.

The latter, 'Belladonna',
Connects the flower to the witch,
It translates as 'beautiful lady',
Both allure and both bewitch.

She would use the deadly nightshade,
And the berries they produced,
To lace the wine of sailors,
Where the toxic plant induced.

It hallucinate its victims,
And would blur the sailors' sight,
They consumed the potent flower,
Which would then expend their fight.

Circe watch as each relinquish,
They suppress, concede, and quell,
Now the deadly nightshades venom,
Has subdued them for her spell.

MOLY

The bell-shaped flowers, as white as milk,
Grew unwelcome in her wood,
A unique flower called 'moly',
For her magic it withstood.

A giant named Picolous,
Had fled to Circe's Isle,
Where he terrified the goddess,
Who remained there in exile.

When the sun god heard his daughter,
As she screamed in fear and pain,
He brought down the wrath of fury,
And by his hand, the giant was slain.

Picolous fell upon the land,
As blood poured from his wound,
And as it spilled upon the soil,
A moly sprang and bloomed.

'Moly' derives from 'Molybdenum',
A metal, silver-white,
Insusceptible to many things,
And portrays their arduous fight.

Circe watch as he lay dying,
Then she saw the bloom unfold,
Unaware that it would counteract,
The magic that she hold.

ODYSSEUS

Odysseus, the king of Ithaca,
Anchored down on Circe's Isle,
Once he learnt that she transformed his crew,
He resolved to reconcile.

Hermes gifted him with Moly,
As the God of luck then say:
'Her magic it shall counteract,
Go forth, be on your way!'

Odysseus reached the witch's house,
Where she offered him some wine,
Intent to cast her magic spell,
And turn the king to swine.

The goddess swiftly pulled her wand,
Out from her ample chest,
As the king retrieved his mighty sword,
And pressed it to her breast.

Unaware he carried Moly,
The witch fell to his feet,
'The only man' she wept and wailed,
'My spell cannot defeat'.

She was fearful but in awe of him,
And swore upon the blade,
To return his men and hide her wand,
For however long he stayed.

ONE YEAR

A prophecy once spoke of you,
And your visit to Aeaea,
I shall offer you much pleasure sir,
If you stay with me a year.

One single year is all I ask,
My Odysseus, I implore,
You stay here with me on the isle,
I shall not ask for more.

I shall hide away my magic,
If you promise you shall stay,
For you, my king, are the only man,
My witchcraft cannot sway.

One year is all I ask of you,
For our bodies to entwine,
I shall tease, appease and please you,
If for twelve months you are mine.

I long to share my bed with you,
Where each night we embrace,
To hold you close in deep repose,
Then awaken to your face.

Odysseus, the year you lose,
Shall be worth the sacrifice,
As your journey home is a treacherous one,
But you shall live, with my advice.

THE WARNING

Come sit with me my darling,
For I have so much to say.
The time has come for you to hear,
Of the perils on your way.

Once you leave Aeaean shores,
The sirens three, shall lure,
I have told them of you long ago,
But I know you shall endure.

You shall pass the land of sirens,
Where two paths lay in wait,
The choice is yours my darling,
Though each hold a different fate.

The Sympleglades are wandering rocks,
That collide when vessels pass,
And none but one survives them,
For they ravage when they clash.

Your alternative route from the sirens,
Shall lead you to two rocks averse,
One is the dwelling of Scylla,
And in the other lives Charybdis.

If you steer your helm right, my Odysseus,
Then it is Scylla the monster you meet,
Six men shall be lost,
For that is her cost,
But the rest shall not suffer defeat.

If you choose to steer left, dear Odysseus,
Then it is Charybdis, the whirlpool you meet,
She gulps down the sea,
Spits it out with fury,
And every man and his vessel deplete.

If you stay to the right, sweet Odysseus,
You shall venture to Hyperion's' Isle,
The God of the sun will allow you to roam,
And to rest from your perilous trial.

But his kindness comes not without caution,
For his sacred flock shall tempt the weak.
If you or your crew come to harm them,
Then the wrath of the Gods, he shall seek.

Suppress any notion of hunger,
And think only of journeying home.
These are the warnings I give you,
In the hope you return to your throne.

ELLIPSISM

My heart compels my mouth to speak,
And beg for you to stay,
But I shall not say the words to you,
I shall watch you sail away.

My heart compels my hands to reach,
And draw you in, close by,
But I shall not grasp your body,
I shall only wave goodbye.

My heart compels my eyes to cry,
And show my tears of grief,
But I shall not cry to guilt you,
I shall hold them till you leave.

My heart compels my mind to think,
And see that which is true,
Ellipsism, uncertainty,
Of a future without you.

SPELLBOUND

She enchanted them, beguiled them,

Possessed them with her grace,

Every man that she encountered,

Lost and spellbound by her face,

Lustful longing overcame them,

By her side they wished to be,

Overwhelmed and overwrought by,

Unequivocal beauty.

No man can break the spell, they are,

Devout, eternally.

ADRIFT

My fingers trace the silhouette,
Of your vessel as you leave,
I longed to ask for you to stay,
But my mouth betrayed my grief.
It did not ask, nor did it beg,
It simply said goodbye,
A broken heart so many times,
Prevented it to try.

Your silhouette is fading,
Ever further from my view,
My eyes then scour the open sea,
For the faintest trace of you.
I promised that I would not cry,
Till your ship was out of sight,
But a broken heart repeatedly,
Had expend my will to fight.

You have gone from me forever,
Only memories remain,
Here I stand upon the island,
In reflection, with disdain.
The absence of you leaving,
Causes thoughts of you to shift,
And a broken heart, without you,
Leaves me aimlessly adrift.

'Do you feel Circe's potency?
Does she offer food and wine?
Be cautious, for the lustful,
Shall be transformed into swine.'

POETRY INDEX

SIREN

OIZYS

APHRODITE

PERSEPHONE

THE FATES

ASTERIA

SELENE

NYX

CIRCE

NOT QUITE READY TO SAY
GOODBYE YET? FOLLOW MY
SOCIALS FOR MORE POETRY:

 @em_doe86

 _emmadoe

Printed in Great Britain
by Amazon

76256165R00151